Free at Last?

**Tom Monaghan
Sam Henry**

Pulse Publications

CONTENTS

1	Slavery in North America	5
2	After World War I: 1918–1924	11
3	African Americans in the 1920s	16
4	The Great Depression and the New Deal	21
5	African Americans in the 1930s	24
6	Changing Times: 1941–1951	33
7	Education: Separate but equal?	38
8	The Montgomery Bus Boycott	42
9	The Southern Christian Leadership Conference	46
10	Malcolm X and the Nation of Islam	49
11	Birmingham, Alabama	53
12	Life in the Ghettos	58
13	Black Power	63
14	Free at Last?	69

ACKNOWLEDGEMENTS
The authors and publishers would like to thank the following for permission to reproduce copyright material:
Hulton-Deutsch pages 8, 9, 10, 11, 13, 15, 16, 17, 18, 21, 22, 23, 24, 25, 29, 30, 31, 33, 34, 35, 36, 37, 39, 40, 44, 45, 46, 47, 49, 50, 52, 54, 57, 59, 60, 61, 62, 65, 66, 68, 71; Pppperfoto photographs on pages 38, 41, 48, 56, 58, 64, 69, 70; The Illustrated London News page 6, 29.

All rights reserved. No part of this publication may be reproduced, stored in a retrieval system, or transmitted in any form or by any means, electronic, mechanical, photocopying, recording or otherwise, without written permission from the publishers.

Published and typeset by
Pulse Publications
45 Raith Road, Fenwick,
Ayrshire, KA3 6DB

Printed and bound by
Thomson Colour Printers

British Library Cataloguing-in-Publication Data
A Catalogue record for this book is available from the
British Library
ISBN 0 948 766 90 5
© Monaghan & Henry 2004

Time Chart

1865	At the end of the Civil War slavery was abolished in the USA.	*(page 6)*
1866	The 14th Amendment to the US Constitution.	*(page 6)*
1870	The 15th Amendment to the US Constitution.	*(page 6)*
1875	Civil Rights Act.	*(page 6)*
1883	US Supreme Court decided that the Civil Rights Act (1875) broke the terms of the US Constitution.	*(page 6)*
1887	Between 1887 and 1891 many southern states introduced Jim Crow laws.	*(page 7)*
1896	US Supreme Court declared that Jim Crow laws were not unconstitutional.	*(page 7)*
1909	National Association for the Advancement of Coloured People (NAACP) was set up.	*(page 10)*
1914	Marcus Garvey set up the Universal Negro Improvement Association in Jamaica and moved to the USA in 1917.	*(page 18)*
1917	USA entered the Great War.	*(page 13)*
1919	Chicago race riots.	*(page 14)*
1920	The 'Red Scare' began.	*(page 14)*
1921	The Quota Act limited immigration from southern and eastern Europe.	*(page 15)*
1924	The National Origins Act made it even more difficult for people from southern and eastern Europe to enter the USA.	*(page 15)*
	Membership of the Ku Klux Klan reached its peak.	*(page 16)*
1927	Sacco and Vanzetti were executed.	*(page 15)*
1929	Wall Street Crash led to worldwide economic depression.	*(page 21)*
	The Nation of Islam was founded in Detroit, Michigan.	*(page 49)*
1931	The Scottsboro Boys case began.	*(page 26)*
1932	Franklin D Roosevelt won the presidential election introducing his 'New Deal' for all Americans in 1933.	*(page 22)*
1936	African American athlete Jesse Owens won four gold medals at the Berlin Olympics.	*(page 29)*
1941	USA entered World War II.	*(page 33)*
	The March on Washington Movement was set up by A Philip Randolph.	*(page 33)*
1942	The Congress of Racial Equality (CORE) was formed.	*(page 36)*
1954	Brown v Topeka Board of Education case.	*(page 39)*
	Arrest of Mrs Rosa Parks led to the Montgomery Bus Boycott in Alabama.	*(page 42)*
	Martin Luther King became the leader of the Montgomery Improvement Association (MIA) that organised the boycott.	*(page 43)*
	Malcolm X joined the Nation of Islam.	*(page 50)*
1957	Nine African American teenagers became students at the Central High School in Little Rock, Arkansas despite racist protests.	*(page 40)*
	The Civil Rights Act was passed.	*(page 46)*
	The Southern Christian Leadership Conference (SCLC) was formed.	*(page 46)*
1960	James Meredith began his campaign to become a student at the Mississippi Law School.	*(page 41)*
	The Student Non-violent Coordinating Committee (SNCC) was set up.	*(page 47)*
	The SNCC began to organise sit-ins and other protests.	*(page 47)*
	CORE began to organise 'Freedom Rides'.	*(page 48)*
1963	Civil rights demonstrations in Birmingham, Alabama.	*(page 54)*
	The March on Washington took place.	*(page 55)*
	The Sixteenth Street Church Bombing took place in Birmingham, Alabama.	*(page 55)*
1964	Civil Rights Act.	*(page 55)*
	Civil rights demonstrations in Selma, Alabama.	*(page 56)*
1965	Malcolm X was murdered in New York.	*(page 51)*
	Voting Rights Act.	*(page 57)*
	The Watts Riots in Los Angeles.	*(page 59)*
1966	The Black Panthers were set up in Oakland, California.	*(page 66)*
1968	Kerner Commission report published.	*(page 61)*
	Martin Luther King was murdered in Memphis, Tennessee.	*(page 69)*
	Civil Rights Act.	*(page 70)*

Glossary

American Dream: the belief that anyone can prosper in the USA if they work hard and use their talents.

Black Panthers: African American organisation founded in San Francisco in 1966; the Black Panthers were popular with many young African Americans living in urban ghettos.

Black Power: the term used by Stokely Carmichael to encourage African Americans to take pride in their African heritage, and to fight for their civil rights; the Black Power symbol was a clenched fist.

Civil rights: basic human rights such as free speech, the right to vote, and freedom from prejudice and discrimination.

Colonies: places where people from one country travel abroad, settle down and create new communities or trading centres.

CORE (1942): Congress of Racial Equality.

Double-V campaign: during World War II, African Americans said that they were fighting for a double victory—against America's enemies and against racism in the USA.

Emancipation Proclamation (1863): when President Abraham Lincoln committed the USA to abolishing slavery when the civil war ended.

FOR: Fellowship of Reconciliation; pacifists who opposed war as a means of solving disputes.

Ghettos: areas of towns or cities where groups of people are forced to live, cut off from the rest of the population; groups of people are kept separate because of their race and/or their religion; ghettos are often poor, run-down and overcrowded.

Great Depression: from 1929 there was a serious slump in international trade leading to a worldwide economic crisis; most countries suffered from factory closures, high unemployment, low prices for farm produce, poverty and political instability.

Great Migration: between 1915 and 1930 nearly one million African Americans moved from the South to work in cities in the north and west of the country.

Immigrants: people who enter a country from another country ito settle down and start a new life.

Jim Crow: a crude stereotype of African Americans based on an elderly slave character who was supposed to have sung and danced for his master; laws denying African Americans their civil rights were called 'Jim Crow' laws.

Ku Klux Klan (KKK): white racist organisation that was founded in 1866, died out in the 1870s, then was revived by WASPs in the 1920s; in the 1920s the KKK was hostile to African Americans, Catholics, Jews and other minority groups.

Kwanzaa: winter festival when African Americans celebrate their African heritage.

Lynching: when a group of people attack and murder victims accused of crimes; lynch mobs act outside the law, pay little or no attention to gathering evidence, and deny victims their civil rights.

MIA (1954): Montgomery Improvement Association; its first leader was Martin Luther King.

Motown: Detroit, Michigan, the motor town (due to its large number of car manufacturers); important centre of African American music in the 1960s and 1970s.

MOWM (1941): the March on Washington Movement founded by A Philip Randolph.

NAACP: National Association for the Advancement of Coloured People.

New Deal: term used to describe the programme of reforms introduced by President Franklin D Roosevelt after 1933 to deal with the problems caused by the Great Depression.

Open Door policy: when the USA allowed hundreds of thousands of immigrants from anywhere in the world to enter the country.

Quota System: in the 1920s the USA restricted the number of immigrants from different countries according to how many people from each country lived in the USA, first in 1910, and then in 1890, to cut the number of immigrants from southern and eastern Europe.

Red Scare: when the US government believed that American freedom and democracy were under threat from Communists and other groups of revolutionaries; red was seen as the colour of Communism.

SCLC (1957): Southern Christian Leadership Conference; important civil rights group.

Segregation: keeping people apart; forcing some people to endure inferior and degrading conditions while other people enjoy luxury; dividing people according to their race and colour.

Slavery: when people are forced to work for an owner who can buy and sell them as his or her own property.

SNCC (1960): Student Non-violent Coordinating Committee; organised sit-ins and other protests.

Trade: buying and selling farm produce, manufactured goods and natural resources such as coal and oil.

UNIA: Universal Negro Improvement Association.

Wall Street Crash (1929): economic crisis in the USA that marked the beginning of the Great Depression that lasted until the outbreak of World War II.

WASPs: White Anglo-Saxon Protestants; the most powerful group of people in the USA.

Free at Last?

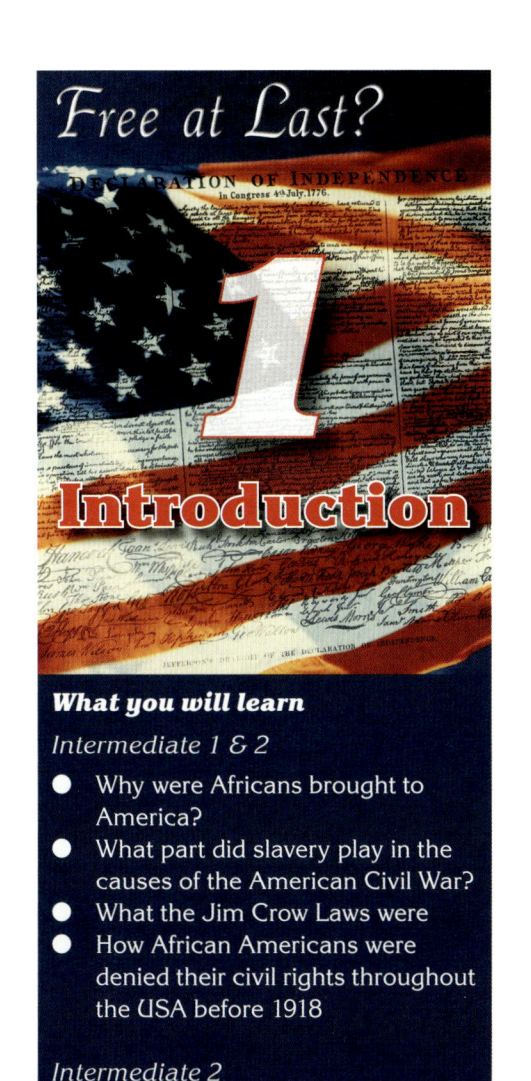

1 Introduction

What you will learn

Intermediate 1 & 2
- Why were Africans brought to America?
- What part did slavery play in the causes of the American Civil War?
- What the Jim Crow Laws were
- How African Americans were denied their civil rights throughout the USA before 1918

Intermediate 2
- The work of W E B Du Bois and Booker T Washington

SLAVERY IN NORTH AMERICA

The United States of America is a land of immigrants. From the late fifteenth century (i.e. the late 1400s), different parts of the land which became the USA were explored and settled by the Spanish, French, English and Dutch. By the seventeenth century (the 1600s), Britain was establishing colonies along the Atlantic coast and was beginning a trade with Africa. This led to African captives being brought to the American colonies to work as slaves. These slaves were used chiefly as farm labour to produce crops such as tobacco, sugar, cotton and rice. These crops were sold by the colonists to Britain.

When the thirteen American colonies broke away from Britain to become independent, the Declaration of Independence, signed in 1776, stated that "all men are created equal". American citizens were promised certain "inalienable rights", including the rights to "life, liberty and the pursuit of happiness", but African American slaves remained slaves. Soon after the colonies became the United States of America, Eli Whitney's invention of the cotton gin or engine in 1793 resulted in a huge growth in cotton production. This led to an increase in slave numbers to over 4 million by 1860, even though importing African captives had been banned in 1808.

In the first decades of the nineteenth century, there was growing opposition to slavery in the northern states where there were few if any slaves. Northerners saw farmers who employed slave labour in the southern states as having an economic advantage over those in the north whose labourers were free. Also, north-

1. New Hampshire
2. Massachussetts
3. Rhode Island
4. Connecticut
5. New Jersey
6. Delaware
7. Maryland

erners were concerned at the political power of the southern slave owners who wanted to use slaves in the new territory being acquired in the west as the USA grew larger. Even though northerners did not regard African Americans as being in any way equal to white Americans, they became concerned about the growth of slavery and its expansion into the west. Tension grew between those for and those against slavery in the southern and northern states in the 1840s and 1850s.

THE AMERICAN CIVIL WAR

The election of Abraham Lincoln as President in 1860 increased fears in the slave-owning states that Lincoln would hinder or even prevent the extension of slavery in the west. This led most slave-owning states to leave the Union. The refusal of Lincoln to accept the secession of these slave states in the South resulted in the outbreak of a bloody civil war.

The American Civil War began on 12 April 1861 and lasted four long years until 1865. The slaughter on both sides was considerable. During the war, Lincoln committed the North to abolishing slavery when he issued the Emancipation Proclamation in January 1863. The 13th Amendment to the Constitution, passed in 1865, confirmed this freedom from slavery.

The 14th Amendment (1866) and the 15th Amendment (1870) ensured that all people born or naturalised in the USA were citizens of the USA and that African Americans had the right to vote, whether they lived in the South or the North. A *Civil Rights Act* in 1875 tried to stop segregation in public places.

President Abraham Lincoln, photographed in 1863

PROBLEMS FACING AFRICAN AMERICANS BEFORE 1918

Between 1875 and 1917 when the USA joined the First World War, the civil rights of African Americans were attacked by white racist politicians. In 1883 the United States Supreme Court decided that the 1875 *Civil Rights Act* was unconstitutional. In other words, it broke the rules set out in the Constitution agreed when the United States was set up by the thirteen colonies that fought for and won their independence from Britain. Increasingly, it was accepted that individual states could decide on their own internal affairs without interference from the President and the federal government in Washington DC. This would include issues such as voting rights or the qualifications needed to be able to vote. The white politicians who controlled the governments of southern states introduced racist policies that discriminated against African Americans.

In the 1890s, many states introduced voting qualifications to prevent African Americans from being able to vote. A number of states brought in literacy qualifications for voters. At this time about 2.5 million African Americans in the southern states were illiterate, so they were prevented from using their right to vote. Other regulations placing restrictions on African Americans of voting age resulted in a huge drop in the number of African American voters. In Louisiana in 1900, only 5,320 African Americans were registered to vote, but four years earlier there had been over 130,000 African American voters registered.

Jim Crow Laws and 'separate but equal'

Between 1887 and 1891, many southern states introduced Jim Crow laws. These laws were passed to segregate African Americans from white Americans. Jim Crow laws led to separate schools and hospitals, and separate areas on buses and trains for African Americans and white Americans. African Americans were prevented from using the same facilities as Whites in theatres, restaurants and public baths. In the *American Magazine* in 1908, Ray Stannard Baker described segregation on the streetcars of the southern city of Atlanta, Georgia:

> *"Over the door of each car, I found the sign, 'White people will seat from the front of car toward the back and coloured people from back toward the front'. Sure enough, I found the white people in front and the Negroes (African Americans) behind.*
>
> *The very first time I was on a car in Atlanta, I saw the conductor—all conductors are white—ask a Negro woman to get up and take a seat farther back in order to make a place for a white man. I have also seen white men requested to leave the Negro section of the car."*

In 1896, the legal case of Plessy v Ferguson led to the US Supreme Court stating that segregation was not unconstitutional meaning that Jim Crow laws did not deny African Americans their civil rights as guaranteed by the US Constitution. Jim Crow laws were upheld as being lawful, provided that the separate services were of equal quality and standard—'separate but equal' in the eyes of the Supreme Court. Since it ignored the fact that education, medical services and other facilities were anything but equal, 'separate but equal' facilities allowed discrimination to continue, and often increase.

Lynching

Racist violence was common in the South before the First World War. Lynchings were a common form of assault on African American communities by white racists. Lynchings took place when white mobs attacked and murdered African Americans who were suspected or accused of a crime, and who were often in custody awaiting trial. Frequently, the evidence against these victims was flimsy or non-existent. Local police or sheriffs were powerless to stop these lynch mobs, even when they believed that the victim deserved a fair trial.

Lynching was seen as a justified punishment for crimes such as rape or sexual assault. However, the reality was that even answering back or looking at a white person the wrong way, or being impudent enough to whistle at a white woman might be taken as an excuse to find a victim. Often the victim was tortured before being hung from a tree or even burned alive. Not all the victims were men. In the period before 1918, over fifty victims of lynch mobs were women, some of whom were pregnant at the time.

Although not all lynch mob victims were African American, the overwhelming proportion were. African Americans were the victims in nearly 90% of lynchings.

Poverty in the South

It must be remembered that while the African American community was undoubtedly poor, there were large numbers of Whites in the South who also suffered from poverty. At the start of the twentieth century, the average wage in the South was $500 while in the USA as a whole it was $1,100. Southern factory workers, mainly women and children, were exploited and paid very low wages. They lived in poor quality housing and received a very poor edu-

---

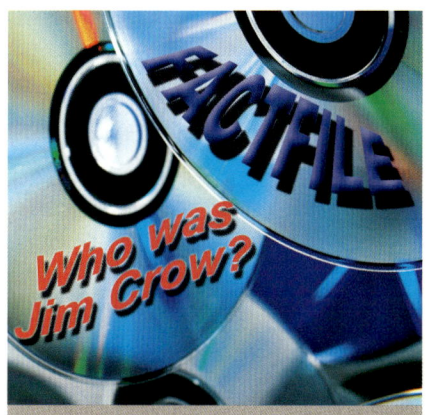

FACTFILE: Who was Jim Crow?

Jim Crow was a clown character played by a white entertainer called Thomas D Rice who pretended to be an African American slave. Rice played the character on stage for the first time in 1828. Jim Crow was supposed to be an elderly slave who sang and danced as he worked for his master. The character was used as a crude stereotype of all African Americans during the rest of the nineteenth century.

cation. Some 12% of the white population in the South were illiterate.

These poor Whites were also denied the right to vote because the discriminatory laws aimed at preventing African Americans from voting made literacy and the ownership of property necessary qualifications to vote.

African Americans in the North

Although the mass movement of African Americans from the southern states to the northern states did not get underway until the first decades of the twentieth century, there were significant numbers of African Americans in northern cities during the nineteenth century. Conditions for African Americans in the northern states, although possibly slightly better than in the South, were harsh and there was still considerable discrimination.

African Americans were able to vote although they often faced threats when they tried to use their rights. Their growing numbers in many northern towns and cities caused concern to the white population who often worried that the votes of African Americans could determine the outcome of local council and mayoral elections.

Usually there was no legal basis for discrimination in the northern states, but in practice African Americans often found it just as difficult to use restaurants and other public places as they did in the South. Often African Americans were prevented from seeking and taking up skilled work. Racially motivated employers, trade unions and the racism of many immigrant groups meant that only the most unskilled and poorly paid jobs were available to African Americans.

By 1917, all large northern cities had black ghettos. These were particular areas of the cities where the African American population was forced to live. They were typified as being poor, run-down, overcrowded and unhealthy. Housing was the cheapest available and the most basic. They were unsanitary and infant mortality was especially high. Violent crime was common in these areas as they tended to suffer from poor policing.

From time to time there were incidents of inter-racial violence

A crowd gathering to witness the killing of Thomas Shipp and Abram Smith, two victims of lynch law in Indiana. (See page 27)

in the North. Springfield, the state capital of Illinois was the scene of one such incident in 1908. Violent clashes between the white and African American communities resulted in the deaths of four white men. Reprisals were carried out. Two African Americans were lynched and over one hundred people were injured.

Clearly, whether they lived in the South or in the North, African Americans were subjected to a great deal of discrimination and violence in the USA before the First World War. While this was true, there were some who were prepared to speak out against these injustices and who laid the foundations of the modern civil rights movement of the second half of the twentieth century. Booker T Washington and WEB Du Bois were two prominent spokespeople for the African American community.

Biographical note: Booker T Washington

Born in 1856 to an African American mother who was a slave, Booker T Washington was given the chance of an education by the wife of a mine owner who employed him as a houseboy or servant. He enrolled as a student at the Hampton Agricultural Institute in 1872. After this he became a teacher and in 1888 founded the Tuskegee Negro National Institute in Alabama to provide academic and vocational training for African Americans. This institute or college was intended to give young African Americans practical skills in occupations such as farming and carpentry. The institute became a world famous centre for agricultural research and received the support of white people who were willing to provide financial help for its work. Washington believed African Americans would gain the respect of white Americans through hard work and education, and that African Americans would show themselves to be responsible and reliable citizens.

Booker T Washington founded the National Negro Business League in 1900. This organisation was set up to provide support and encouragement for African American businessmen. In 1915 there were 600 branches of the League across the USA.

Booker T Washington was highly regarded by Presidents Theodore Roosevelt and William Taft in the early twentieth century. They consulted him on African American affairs. Washington's views brought him into conflict with other African American leaders. His critics said that he appeared to be prepared to accept a lower status for African Americans compared to white Americans. They also said that he was willing to accept that African Americans should not demand an end to segregation, nor demand rights which were equal to those of white Americans. He died in 1915.

Biographical note: W E B du Bois

William Edward Burghardt Du Bois was born in 1868. He graduated from Fisk University in 1885, spent two years studying in Berlin, and then studied African American history at Harvard University back in the USA. In 1895 he was the first African American to receive a Doctorate of Philosophy from Harvard University. He then went to teach Economics and History at Atlanta University in Georgia

Du Bois demanded full civil rights for African Americans, an end to racial segregation, the restoration of the right to vote for African Americans, and greater equality of opportunity for all African Americans. In 1909 he joined with other African Americans to set up the National Association for the Advancement of Coloured People (NAACP). The NAACP's chief aims were to inform Americans of both good and bad things that were happening to African Americans and to help improve the lives of African Americans.

Du Bois edited the NAACP magazine *Crisis* from 1910. This enjoyed a wide readership, with a circulation of over 100,000 by 1919. He campaigned against Jim Crow laws, lynchings and sexual inequality. *Crisis* regularly published horrific photographs of lynch victims to publicise the effects of racism on ordinary people.

Du Bois had very different views from Booker T Washington. Du Bois was outspoken in his support for justice and equal rights for African Americans, and he was not prepared to keep quiet in the way that Booker T Washington did.

As well as editing *Crisis*, Du Bois wrote more than twenty books. His most popular book was *The Souls of Black Folks,* published in 1903. In old age Du Bois moved to Ghana in West Africa and died there two years later in 1963.

Free at Last?

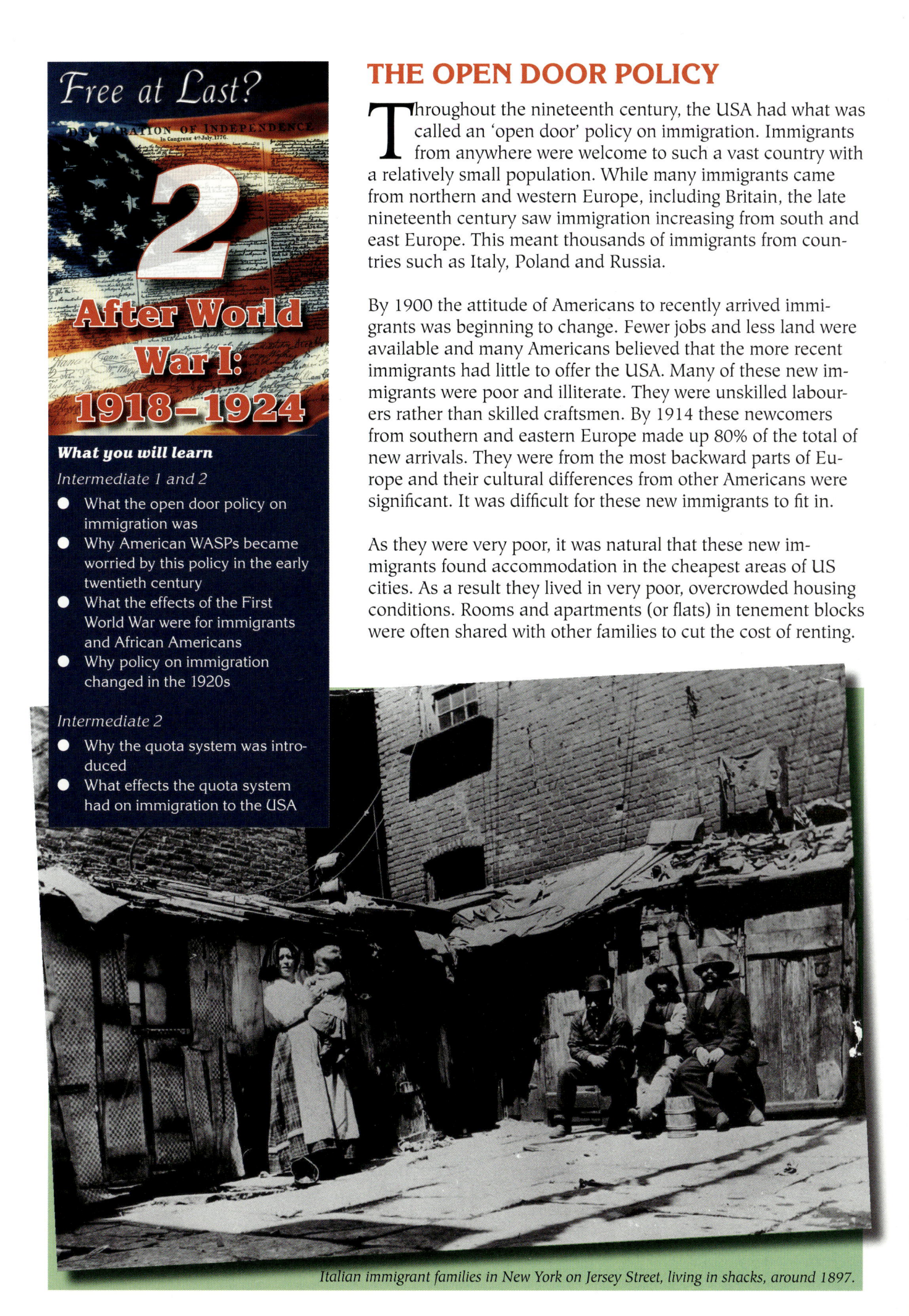

2 After World War I: 1918–1924

What you will learn

Intermediate 1 and 2
- What the open door policy on immigration was
- Why American WASPs became worried by this policy in the early twentieth century
- What the effects of the First World War were for immigrants and African Americans
- Why policy on immigration changed in the 1920s

Intermediate 2
- Why the quota system was introduced
- What effects the quota system had on immigration to the USA

THE OPEN DOOR POLICY

Throughout the nineteenth century, the USA had what was called an 'open door' policy on immigration. Immigrants from anywhere were welcome to such a vast country with a relatively small population. While many immigrants came from northern and western Europe, including Britain, the late nineteenth century saw immigration increasing from south and east Europe. This meant thousands of immigrants from countries such as Italy, Poland and Russia.

By 1900 the attitude of Americans to recently arrived immigrants was beginning to change. Fewer jobs and less land were available and many Americans believed that the more recent immigrants had little to offer the USA. Many of these new immigrants were poor and illiterate. They were unskilled labourers rather than skilled craftsmen. By 1914 these newcomers from southern and eastern Europe made up 80% of the total of new arrivals. They were from the most backward parts of Europe and their cultural differences from other Americans were significant. It was difficult for these new immigrants to fit in.

As they were very poor, it was natural that these new immigrants found accommodation in the cheapest areas of US cities. As a result they lived in very poor, overcrowded housing conditions. Rooms and apartments (or flats) in tenement blocks were often shared with other families to cut the cost of renting.

Italian immigrant families in New York on Jersey Street, living in shacks, around 1897.

This is the main reception hall on Ellis Island where all immigrants from Europe were processed. Today it is a national museum remembering the millions of people who entered the USA through New York. Below is a drawing of immigrants seeing the Statue of Liberty for the first time as they approach Ellis Island.

Windows were ill-fitting, roofs leaked, sanitation was poor, and disease and death rates were high.

Usually groups of newly arrived immigrants moved into areas of American cities where fellow nationals lived. All the major cities developed separate national areas often called 'Little Italy', 'Little Poland' or 'Little Russia'. These were separate ghetto areas for Italians, Poles and Jews where these groups kept their own language, as well as their own cultural and religious traditions. In time, they set up their own shops, churches and schools. As a result, many Americans felt cut off from these areas.

These poor immigrants were willing to take on the dirty and dangerous jobs which nobody else wanted in factories and workplaces. In particular, women were willing to take jobs in 'sweat shops', working long hours for extremely low wages in the textile and garment industries, sewing on shirt buttons, and so on. This willingness to take badly paid jobs, and their acceptance of poor living and working conditions, earned the new immigrants the anger of native-born Americans who felt that these immigrants were responsible for keeping wages low and working conditions poor. Employers knew they could always use cheap immigrant labour to break strikes organised by American trade unions.

WASPs

This led to the growth of what was called 'nativism'. White Protestant Americans whose families originally came from northern or western European countries such as England (known as WASPs or White Anglo-Saxon Protestants) believed in their own superiority over other nationalities and they were determined to maintain their racial superiority. The WASPs claimed to be descended from the original settlers and founders of the colonies that became the United States, although many were the children or grandchildren of nineteenth century immigrants. The WASPs despised the lifestyle of the newcomers. They despised the new immigrants' cultural traditions and were suspicious of their political beliefs and activities.

A group of African American soldiers returning home from Europe after World War I. They are all wearing the Croix de Guerre (Cross of War) of France, which they were awarded for bravery in battle.

FACTFILE: African Americans in World War I

African Americans could not become US marines in the First World War, nor could they become officers in the US navy. The 1,400 African American officers in the US army were assigned mostly to labour battalions rather than front-line duties. Hundreds of African American servicemen wrote letters of protest to the US Secretary of War complaining about discrimination and prejudice in the armed forces.

However, the 369th Infantry Regiment had the best record of any US army regiment in the First World War. This all-African American regiment was known by other regiments as the 'Harlem Hell Fighters'. Henry Johnson and Needham Roberts of the 369th regiment killed or wounded more than twenty German soldiers who had tried to make a surprise attack on the regiment's position. Both soldiers were awarded the Croix de Guerre for outstanding bravery by the French government.

Also, the WASPs suspected that the newcomers were prepared to use violence to get their way and take control of the USA.

In addition, the new immigrants spoke different languages and many were either Catholics or Jews. Protestant Americans felt fearful and intimidated, and this fear was seen in the growth of anti-Catholic and anti-Jewish organisations, and in groups campaigning for an end to immigration, or for restrictions on immigration from certain parts of Europe. In 1917, acting on the results of a government enquiry a decade earlier, literacy tests for new immigrants were introduced to reduce the number of ill-educated and often poor immigrants.

THE FIRST WORLD WAR

At first, the USA remained neutral during the Great War that broke out in Europe in 1914. Feelings about the war were mixed as a result of the multicultural nature of American society. Some people supported Britain, while those of German, Austrian or Hungarian descent were sympathetic towards Germany and its allies. Most Americans thought that neutrality made sense and that the USA could benefit from supplying both sides with materials for the war. However, in April 1917 the USA entered the war on the side of Britain, France and Russia. This was to have a considerable impact on American attitudes to immigrants and African Americans.

Suspicion grew towards certain groups whose origins were European. German Americans faced hostility which was to last for some time after the war had ended. Boycotts of German businesses were organised. A lot of the opposition to the war within the United States came from immigrant communities. Italian Americans were especially opposed to the war. A number of what were known as anarchist groups with roots in the Italian American community organised strikes for better wages. These groups began to criticise the war. One Italian publication caused so much concern that its editor, Luigi Galleani, and his colleagues were arrested and deported at the end of the war.

African Americans were also affected by the war. The expansion of industry as a result of the war resulted in huge numbers of African Americans moving to northern cities from the rural southern states looking for factory jobs. Around a half a million African Americans moved north to cities such as New York, Chicago, Philadelphia, Boston, Detroit and St Louis during the war years. Immigration was also difficult during the war years so African Americans benefited from the job opportunities created. Whole areas of cities such as Harlem in New York became African American ghettos which were to remain after the war ended.

370,000 African Americans joined the US armed forces and served overseas during the First World War. This experience made them more aware of the discrimination they had to put up with at home. On their return they were more determined than ever to demand greater equality.

At the end of the war in 1918, those serving in the forces returned to their homes. White Americans discovered that their jobs had been taken by African Americans and parts of their cities had also been taken over by them. This led to considerable competition for jobs and housing and this, in turn, led to anger and violence.

THE CHICAGO RACE RIOTS

In July 1919 problems were created by growing tension between returning soldiers and the African American population in Chicago. The number of African Americans in Chicago had increased by 50,000 during the war. As in many other areas of life, beaches on the shore of Lake Michigan were segregated with whites-only beaches. A teenage African American wandered towards a whites-only beach. White people on the beach began to throw stones at him and continued to do so until he drowned.

As a result of his death there were thirteen days of rioting and violence during which Irish and Polish workers attacked the black ghettos in the city. Twenty three African Americans and fifteen white Americans were killed. More than 500 people were injured and over 1,000 families, mainly African American, were left homeless.

Although the Chicago riots were one of the worst instances of racial violence there were others like them in more than twenty cities across the USA. In Tulsa, Oklahoma, in 1921, African American residents attempted to prevent a member of their community from being lynched by white residents. This led to a massacre of African Americans the scale of which only became public knowledge many years later. The African American community in Tulsa was virtually eliminated by white racist violence in the 1920s.

THE RED SCARE

In 1917, there was a revolution in Russia which led to the Bolsheviks or Communists gaining power after a brief but bloody civil war. There was a fear in the United States that Communists might also try to overthrow the American government. This fear was heightened by the fact that there was a huge wave of strikes in America in 1919. Strikes and trade union activities appeared to many WASPs to be a dangerous un-American development. Mitchell Palmer, the United States Attorney General whose house had been bombed by some terrorists, tried to rid the country of people whom he called "foreign subversives and agitators" during what was known as the 'Red Scare'. (Communists were known as 'Reds' because their symbol was the red flag.)

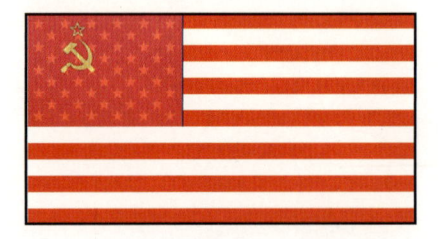

Italian-born anarchists and convicted murderers Bartolomeo Vanzetti (1888–1927) (C) and Nicola Sacco (1891–1927) (R) sit handcuffed to a guard in Dedham, Massachusetts. They were executed in Boston in 1927 for the murders of two men during a robbery. In 1977, Governor Michael S Dukakis exonerated them.

SACCO AND VANZETTI

An important example of growing hostility towards new immigrants was the case of Nicola Sacco and Bartolomeo Vanzetti. They were Italians who belonged to a political group known as anarchists. Also, they knew Luigi Galleani who had been deported earlier by Mitchell Palmer. The anarchists had opposed entry into the First World War, had avoided military service in the US armed forces, and they had supported workers' strikes during the war. In 1920 Sacco and Vanzetti were charged with the murder of two messengers and the theft of over $15,000 from the Slater and Morrill Shoe Factory in Massachusetts.

Sacco and Vanzetti were arrested at the height of the 'Red Scare' action against aliens started by Mitchell Palmer. Their trial was not a fair one. The Judge, Webster Thayer, was clearly prejudiced against them because they were Italian immigrants and because they were involved in political activities. They were convicted on evidence that was highly suspect, and evidence in their defence was ignored. Finally, when both men were executed in 1927, there were protests throughout the USA and in Europe.

On 1 January 1920 around 6,000 people were arrested and imprisoned. This round-up of foreigners was organised by a young civil servant called J Edgar Hoover who later became one of the most powerful men in the USA as Director of the Federal Bureau of Investigation, or FBI. More than 500 of these people were forced to leave the country. The killing of thirty eight people by a terrorist bomb in Wall Street, New York, in September 1920 encouraged individual states to carry out similar measures against 'aliens'.

THE QUOTA SYSTEM

As a result of increasing hostility towards immigrants in the 1920s new laws were passed restricting the number of immigrants who could enter the USA. *The Quota Act* of 1921 limited immigration from eastern and southern Europe. A quota system was introduced. This quota was fixed at 3% per year of the total number of people from each different nationality group living in the USA in 1910. *The National Origins Act* of 1924 took the Quota Act a stage further. The quota was reduced to 2% and was applied to the population as it had been calculated in 1890. Since immigration from southern and eastern Europe had grown considerably after that date, people from these areas found it more difficult to enter the USA. In addition, immigrants of Asian origin, who were mainly Chinese or Japanese, were prevented by the new law from entering the USA at all.

The quota system severely limited the number of Italian and Polish immigrants allowed into the USA. As well as these mainly Catholic groups, few Russian Jews were allowed to come to America. Poor, unskilled and often illiterate immigrants also faced another kind of discrimination. Trained and talented people such as actors, musicians, nurses and people trained in the professions such as medicine and law could enter from any country. It was the poor and uneducated from eastern and southern Europe who were to be kept out at all costs.

Free at Last?

3
African Americans in the 1920s

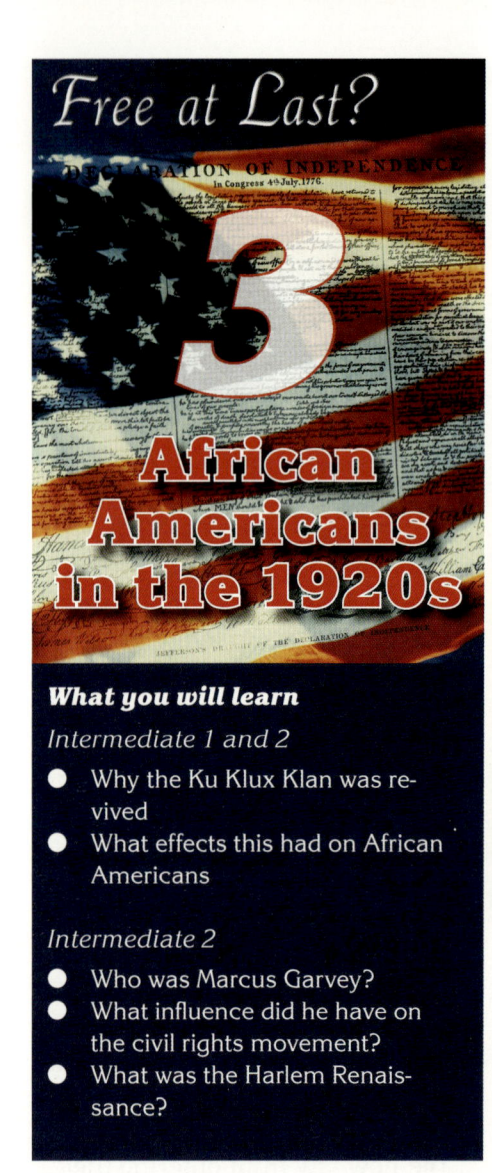

What you will learn

Intermediate 1 and 2
- Why the Ku Klux Klan was revived
- What effects this had on African Americans

Intermediate 2
- Who was Marcus Garvey?
- What influence did he have on the civil rights movement?
- What was the Harlem Renaissance?

THE KU KLUX KLAN REVIVED

The Ku Klux Klan reformed in Georgia in 1915. Its revival was helped by a film, *The Birth of the Nation*, directed by DW Griffith. It was set in the southern states after the Civil War and the abolition of slavery. This film showed the Ku Klux Klan or KKK saving white families from groups of African Americans intent on rape and looting. It attracted huge audiences and undoubtedly revived interest in the KKK. It has been claimed that membership of the KKK at its peak reached as many as four to eight million between 1923 and 1924. Members included state governors and senators as well as judges, sheriffs and members of police forces.

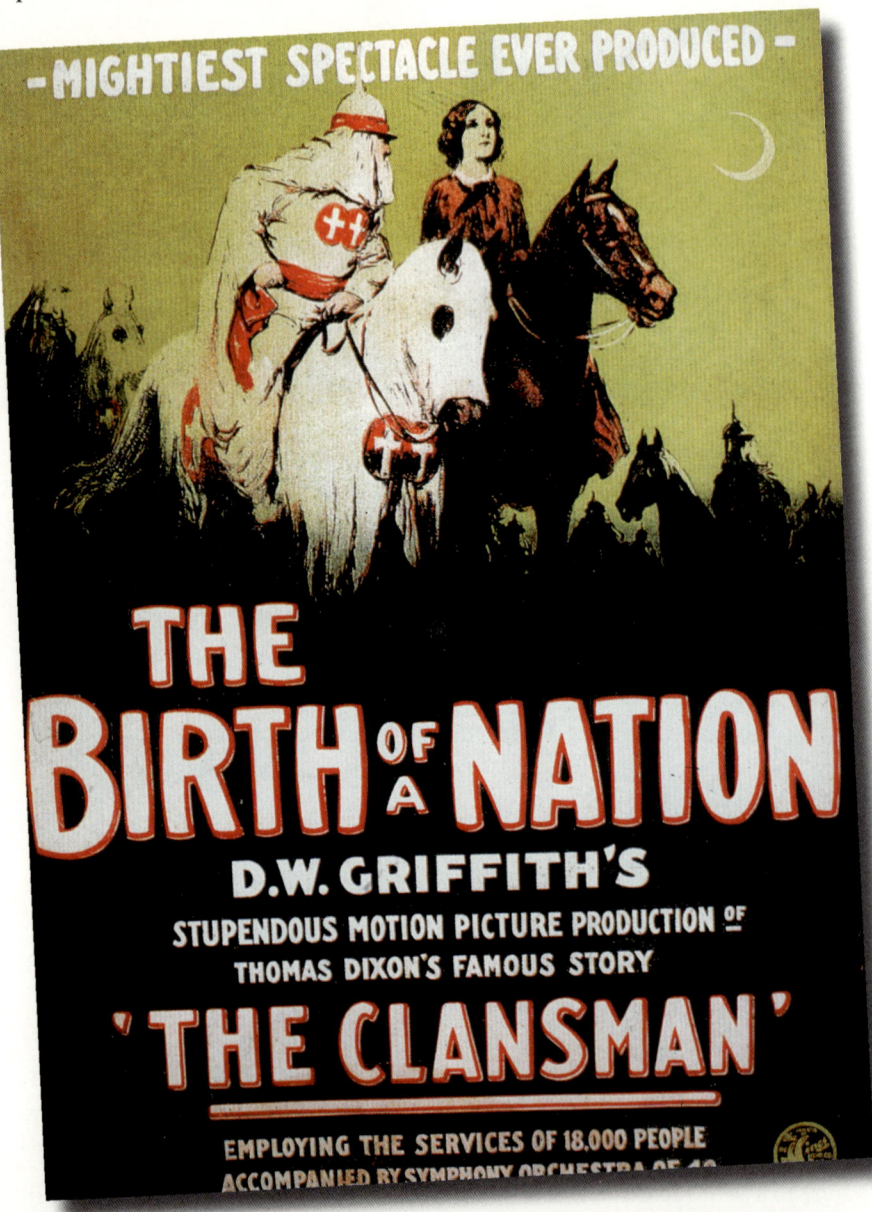

The old methods of beating, lynching, mutilation and murder were carried on as before in the South against African Americans. However, this time the KKK was opposed to immigrants who were Catholics or Jews, and was also against anyone who supported socialism or communism. It claimed to stand for WASP or white Anglo-Saxon Protestant America. One commentator at the time noted:

"It may be asked why did the town take so enthusiastically to the Klan? Many old stock Americans believed they were in danger of being overrun. The 'foreigners were ruling the country'; and so anything 'foreign' was 'un-American' and a menace. Another important idea in American history was anti-Catholicism because many of the founding fathers had come to America to escape Catholic persecutions in Europe."

The Klan held impressive shows of force, with members on parade dressed in their white robes. One observer described a KKK parade in one town in this way:

"Cars were draped with flags and some carried home-made signs with Klan slogans such as 'America for the Americans'. That night there was a parade down Main Street in Kokomo. There were thirty bands. They rolled the slow, heavy tempo of the march to a low meadow where the Klan had put up a twenty five foot 'fiery cross'. Many of the marchers carried flaming torches. Flag bearers usually carried two Klan flags, flanking an American flag, and the word would ripple down the rows of spectators lining the kerbs, 'Here comes the flag!' and 'Hats off for the flag!'."

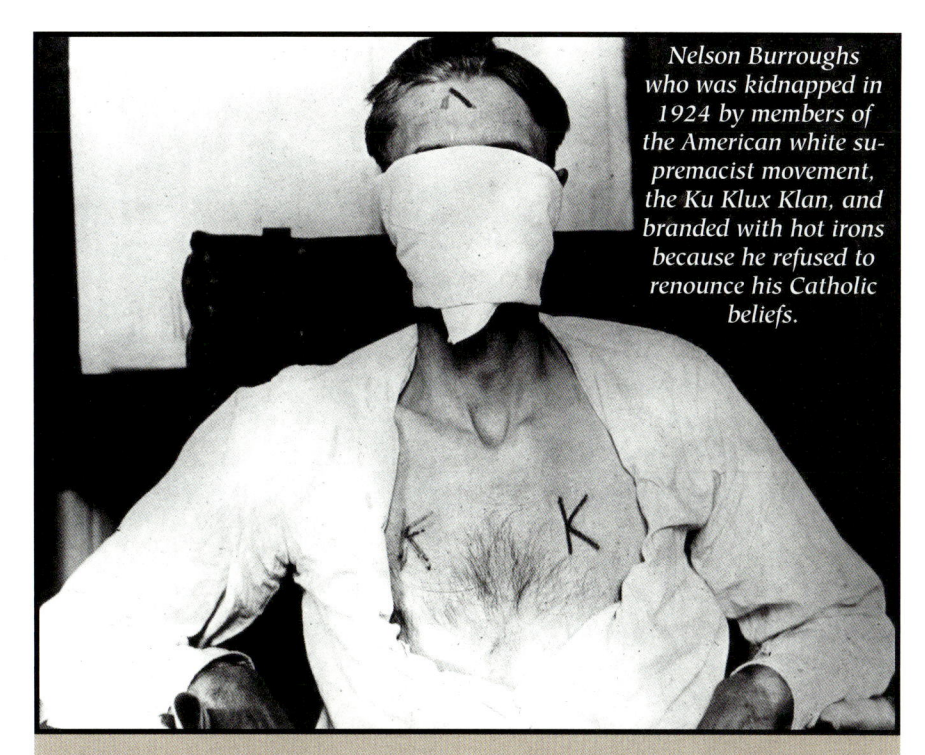

Nelson Burroughs who was kidnapped in 1924 by members of the American white supremacist movement, the Ku Klux Klan, and branded with hot irons because he refused to renounce his Catholic beliefs.

The Ku Klux Klan was founded in 1866 by Nathan Bedford Forrest. The KKK opposed equality for former slaves and their families. The KKK attacked and often killed African Americans who tried to stand up for their rights. Attacks usually took place at night and involved groups of Klansmen whose identities were hidden behind the hooded robes worn by members of the KKK. The Klansmen left behind burning crosses as signs of their activities. Pauli Murray talked of her grandparents' experience of the Klan just after the Civil War:

"Late at night she was awakened by the thudding of horses' hooves as nightriders, brandishing torches and yelling like banshees, swept into the clearing and rode round and round her cabin. She never knew when they might set fire to the place, burning her to death inside, and some nights she was so terrified that she would get out of bed, creep through the woods to the roadway and trudge the twelve miles to Durham, preferring the dark, lonely but open road to the risk of being trapped in the farm."

The KKK was only one of a number of white racist organisations to be set up after the Civil War. Although the KKK was formally disbanded in 1869, the US Congress passed Enforcement Acts that allowed the federal government to prosecute former members of the KKK who had continued their activities in many areas. By 1872 the KKK had largely been suppressed.

In 1921, the *Washington Eagle* newspaper described the death of an African American male accused of murdering a white woman in Georgia.

"The Negro was taken to a grove, where each one of more than five hundred people, in Ku Klux Klan ceremonial, had placed a pine knot around a stump, and asked if he had anything to say. The pyre (fire) was lit and a hundred men and women, old and young, grandmothers among them, joined hands and danced around while the Negro burned. A big dance was held in a barn nearby that evening in celebration of the burning, many people coming by car from nearby cities to the gala event."

In 1924 the Democratic Party almost chose Al Smith from New York as its candidate for the US Presidency. Smith was a Catholic and there were 103 votes at the Democratic Party convention before an alternative candidate was found. The new candidate was supported by the northern Democrats who would have preferred Smith, and the southern Democrats, many of whom were KKK members, who wanted a WASP candidate. After 1925 the Klan went into a sharp decline as a result of well-publicised scandals about the brutality and corruption of the Klan's leadership. However, in 1928 there was a brief revival in the KKK's fortunes when the Democrats selected Smith to run for the Presidency and Klansmen protested against the possibility of a Catholic President of the USA.

Biographical note — Marcus Garvey

Marcus Garvey was born in Jamaica in 1887. Garvey worked as a printer in Jamaica and he was active in the island's trade union movement. In 1911, while studying in Britain, Garvey was influenced by other non-whites from throughout the British Empire who were active in the struggles of nations which wanted to win their independence from British rule. He was also influenced by the work and ideas of Booker T Washington. Returning to Jamaica, Garvey wrote a book entitled *The Negro Race and its Problems*.

In 1914 Garvey founded an organisation called the Universal Negro Improvement Association (UNIA). The UNIA had financial problems and Garvey moved to the USA in 1917. He set up a branch or chapter of the UNIA in New York, and by 1919 there were more than thirty chapters of the UNIA in the USA.

Garvey believed in what he called 'Race First' which meant that he urged African Americans to take pride in their African heritage. His weekly newspaper *Negro World* was published from 1918 to 1933, and it sponsored African American beauty contests. Garvey refused to carry adverts for skin bleaches, hair straighteners and other products that were popular with many African Americans who were ashamed of their African American appearance. In 1920 Garvey's Negro Factories Corporation was set up to produce goods for African American consumers such as African American dolls for African American children.

Next Garvey set up the Black Star Line. This was a shipping company that was supposed to operate three steamships sailing between the USA, the West Indies and Africa. In 1925 Garvey was arrested and tried for fraud in connection with the Black Star Line. The three ships had soon broken down, and Garvey had lost $800,000 of the money invested in the company by his African American supporters. He was sentenced to five years in prison, but he was pardoned after two years and deported to Jamaica. He remained active in the civil rights movement from his base in London until his death in 1940.

POVERTY AND DISCRIMINATION

Throughout the 1920s, African Americans continued to struggle against poverty. African Americans' average income fell to under $200 a year. In the northern cities white soldiers returning from Europe after the First World War meant that many African Americans lost their jobs and there was a great deal of poverty in the ghettos. The death rate in Harlem among African Americans was 42% higher than in other parts of New York. Discrimination was a fact of life for African Americans as the *Miami Herald* newspaper noted in 1925.

> *"A small monument made a mysterious appearance yesterday morning. An inscription on one side of the monument reads: 'On this spot a few years ago a white man was found who had been tarred and feathered because he had preached social equality to Negroes.' On another side were the words: 'If you are a reckless Negro or a white man who believes in social equality, be advised Dade County don't need you.' "*

By 1928 the estimated population of the USA was 200,000,000. Half of all Americans lived in urban areas. Half of those Americans who lived on farms lived in the southern states. Life expectancy for white American males was 51.65 years, and for white females it was 54.87. Life expectancy for African American males was only 40.45 years, and for African American females it was 38.45 years.

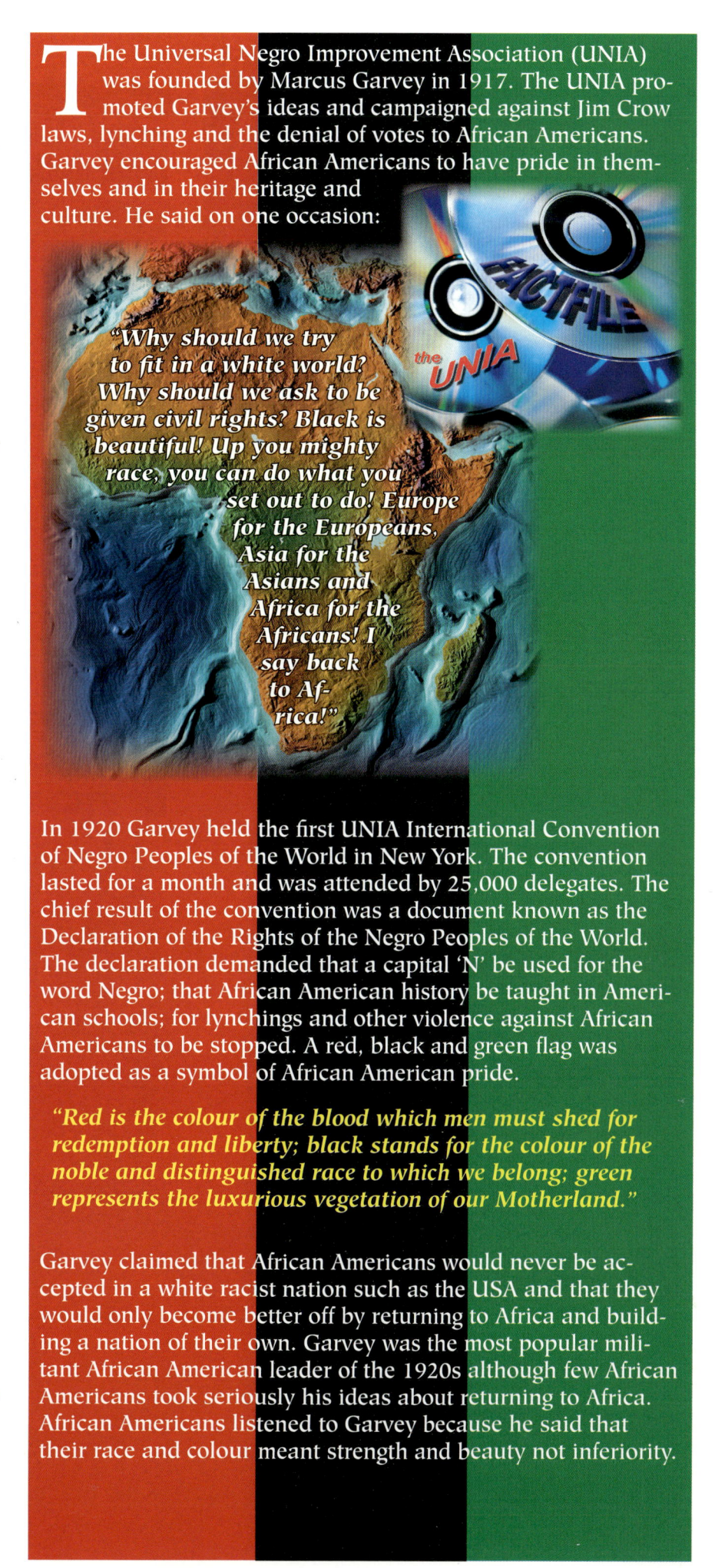

The Universal Negro Improvement Association (UNIA) was founded by Marcus Garvey in 1917. The UNIA promoted Garvey's ideas and campaigned against Jim Crow laws, lynching and the denial of votes to African Americans. Garvey encouraged African Americans to have pride in themselves and in their heritage and culture. He said on one occasion:

> *"Why should we try to fit in a white world? Why should we ask to be given civil rights? Black is beautiful! Up you mighty race, you can do what you set out to do! Europe for the Europeans, Asia for the Asians and Africa for the Africans! I say back to Africa!"*

In 1920 Garvey held the first UNIA International Convention of Negro Peoples of the World in New York. The convention lasted for a month and was attended by 25,000 delegates. The chief result of the convention was a document known as the Declaration of the Rights of the Negro Peoples of the World. The declaration demanded that a capital 'N' be used for the word Negro; that African American history be taught in American schools; for lynchings and other violence against African Americans to be stopped. A red, black and green flag was adopted as a symbol of African American pride.

> *"Red is the colour of the blood which men must shed for redemption and liberty; black stands for the colour of the noble and distinguished race to which we belong; green represents the luxurious vegetation of our Motherland."*

Garvey claimed that African Americans would never be accepted in a white racist nation such as the USA and that they would only become better off by returning to Africa and building a nation of their own. Garvey was the most popular militant African American leader of the 1920s although few African Americans took seriously his ideas about returning to Africa. African Americans listened to Garvey because he said that their race and colour meant strength and beauty not inferiority.

THE HARLEM RENAISSANCE

Poverty and discrimination were not the whole story for African Americans in the 1920s. In the cities African American culture flourished in what became known as the Harlem or Black Renaissance, and the New Negro Movement. African American writers, musicians, performers and artists used their art to express themselves and describe their experiences as African Americans in the USA. African American artists showed new pride in their heritage and cultural traditions.

Renaissance is a term that means 'rebirth' and in the 1920s African Americans' pride in their culture was reborn. African American artists settled in the Harlem district of New York City, together with immigrants from Jamaica, Barbados, Cuba, Puerto Rico, Haiti and other Caribbean countries. In 1925, Alain Locke published *The New Negro* which was a book containing poems, essays, short stories and illustrations which brought to many people's attention the work of African American artists working in Harlem. WEB Du Bois as editor of *Crisis* and A Philip Randolph as editor of *The Messenger* also published the work of African American writers and this helped to inspire other African Americans to become writers and artists.

Jazz was the most popular music among African Americans in the 1920s. Many jazz musicians were based in Harlem where they performed for African American and white audiences. Musicians such as Louis Armstrong, Duke Ellington and Fletcher Henderson were the star musicians of that time. Another popular style of African American music of the 1920s was blues. Blues and jazz had evolved from earlier types of African American music such as work songs, spirituals, ragtime and gospel music. Both styles of music would influence white musicians in the USA, and musicians all over the world, during the rest of the twentieth century.

Biographical note: Florence Mills

Florence Mills was born in Washington D.C. in 1895. She moved to New York in 1910 and together with her sisters she formed a stage act called the Mills Trio. In 1921 Florence took a leading role in the Broadway show *Shuffle Along* and she went on to become the most popular African American entertainer in New York. In 1924 she sang for the first time what became her theme song, *I'm just a little blackbird lookin' for a bluebird*. In 1926 she helped to produce and took part in an all-African American musical revue called *Blackbirds of 1926* which was performed in Harlem, London and Paris. Florence died in 1927 aged thirty-one, and thousands of African Americans lined the streets of Harlem as her funeral procession went past.

Biographical note: Bessie Smith

Bessie Smith was born in 1894. Her first record, *Downhearted blues*, sold more than one million copies in 1923. She became known as the Empress of the Blues, and she was the highest paid African American entertainer in the USA. Her recordings included *The St Louis blues*, *Gimme a pigfoot*, *Empty bed blues* and *Nobody knows you when you're down and out*. Bessie Smith died in 1937 following a car crash. To this day a rumour persists in the USA that Smith died because she was taken to a Whites-only hospital and was turned away. This is not true. She had bled to death before she reached a hospital.

Free at Last?

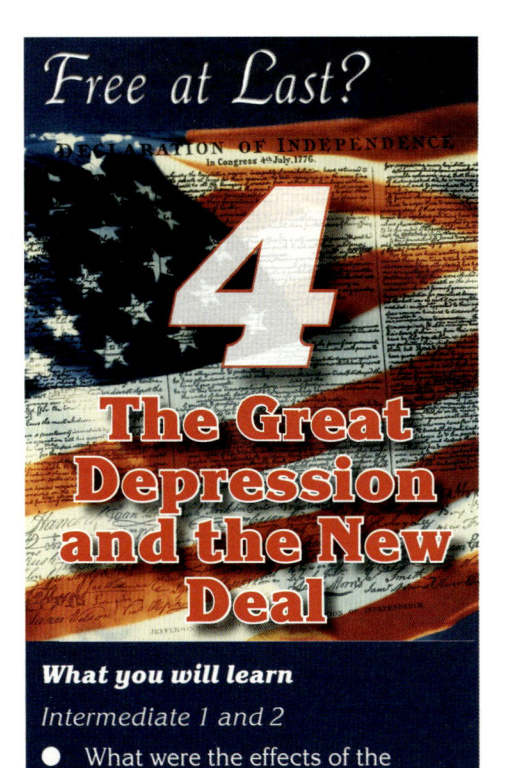

4 The Great Depression and the New Deal

What you will learn

Intermediate 1 and 2
- What were the effects of the Great Depression?
- What was the New Deal?

Intermediate 2
- How important were the Great Migration and the New Deal in the development of the civil rights movement?

THE GREAT DEPRESSION

During the 1920s, despite the fears of the American population that too many immigrants were coming to the USA, the unemployment rate peaked at 6%, and fell as low as 2% in the mid-1920s. Unemployment rose to 9% in 1930 and stood at 24% in 1932—a quarter of the adult population of the USA was unemployed. That meant that there were more than 12 million unemployed Americans looking for work!

After decades of prosperity too many Americans had come to rely on credit and borrowing money to maintain their standard of living. Too many American companies relied on borrowing money to remain in business as their profits fell steadily. In 1929 the value of shares in most American companies collapsed as investors tried to withdraw their investments from the US stock market which was based in Wall Street, New York City.

What became known as the Wall Street Crash in October 1929 led not only to an economic crisis in the USA, but also to a world-wide economic depression that would last until the outbreak of World War II a decade later. Few imports or exports of manufactured goods, high unemployment, falling prices for farm produce, poverty, and political instability were facts of life throughout the developed world in the 1930s.

View of a shanty town and ships taken in 1935, probably located on the banks of the East River in Brooklyn, New York City, during the Great Depression. A man can be seen cooking outdoors on a grill.

POLITICAL INSTABILITY

The Great Depression created genuine fears about the stability of the US political system. Increasing numbers of unemployed and homeless Americans listened to Communist agitators. Demonstrations by the poor and hungry took place in every major city as the American-born and immigrant jobless expressed their anger at the collapse of what was known as the 'American Dream'—the dream that anyone with talent and a capacity for hard work could prosper in the USA. African Americans had known for many years that they were excluded from this dream, but it proved difficult for white Americans to come to terms with the effects of the Great Depression.

Homeless people built temporary or shanty towns called 'Hoovervilles' (at that time the US President was Herbert Hoover) where families lived in tents and huts with no sanitation or other basic facilities. 35,000 demonstrators fought with the police in New York in 1930. In 1932 American First World War veterans formed a Bonus Army of 15,000 men to march on Washington and demand that the cash bonus which was due to be paid to war veterans in 1944 be paid immediately. The Bonus Army's camp in Washington DC was attacked and destroyed by the US army using bayonets and tear gas. Between 1933 and 1935 drought and high winds turned vast areas of the Great Plains into what was called a dust bowl stretching from North Dakota to Texas, ruining farm land and farmers alike. Private armies, including the Khaki Shirts and the Silver Shirts were formed by political extremists across the USA. These armies were modelled on Mussolini's Fascist Blackshirts in Italy and Hitler's Brownshirts in Germany.

A group of men planting trees in 1933 during a Civilian Conservation Corps (CCC) project on the Nett Lake Reservation in Minnesota.

FDR AND THE NEW DEAL

In 1932 the Democratic candidate Franklin Delano Roosevelt (FDR) won the presidential election. He had to wait until March 1933 before he could deliver what he had called his 'New Deal' for the American people. (Roosevelt had the US Constitution amended to move forward the presidential inauguration to the January after the election for all future elections.) In his speech when he was sworn in as US President he said:

> *"First of all, let me assert my firm belief that the only thing we have to fear is fear itself—nameless, unreasoning, unjustified terror which paralyses needed efforts to convert retreat into advance."*

What followed became known as the 'first hundred days' between March and June 1933 when Roosevelt and the US Congress produced a series of laws and other initiatives that one of Roosevelt's supporters said was "the way to put out the fire" that was burning down the USA. Within three months the new president had set up the Federal Emergency Relief Administration, the Civilian Conservation Corps (CCC), Tennessee Valley Authority (TVA), the Public Works Administration, and the National Recovery Administration (NRA). By June 1933 Congress had passed the *Emergency Banking Act*, and the *Agricultural Adjustment Act* that set up the Agricultural Adjustment Administration (AAA) to improve and modernise American farming.

What were called the 'Alphabet Laws' (AAA, CCC, TVA etc.) were supposed to find or create employment for the jobless so that they could earn money to spend on American farm produce and manufactured goods. Other initiatives followed throughout the 1930s although there was no repeat of the flurry of activity during those first one hundred days. These initiatives led to many improvements in the lives of millions of Americans, but they also led to increased government spending and higher taxes.

There is little evidence that large numbers of African Americans voted for FDR and his New Deal before 1936. However, many of the New Deal programmes led to improvements in race relations in the USA, and benefited African American communities across the country. Unlike his wife, President Roosevelt did not hold progressive views on race issues. As a politician President Roosevelt relied on the strength of his Democratic Party in the South where racist politicians and their supporters prevented millions of African Americans from voting. In 1941, the African American leader A Philip Randolph had to threaten to organise a huge march on Washington DC by African Americans to force Roosevelt to do something about racial discrimination in government offices, and in the companies to whom the government awarded contracts.

THE GREAT MIGRATION

The term 'the Great Migration' is often used to describe how nearly one million African Americans moved north to find work in the cities of the North and West between 1915 and 1930. What is less well known is that this migration of African Americans continued throughout the 1930s. For instance, around 150,000 African Americans moved to New York between 1930 and 1940, with most of them settling in Harlem.

Drought, the Dust Bowl, low prices for farm produce, mechanisation, and other agricultural improvements all combined to encourage millions of farmers and agricultural workers to leave the southern states and look for work in the industrial cities of the North. Many of these migrants were poor African Americans who hoped to escape the prejudice and discrimination of the South.

The dramatic social, economic and political changes of the 1920s and 1930s made necessary the rapid growth and development of the civil rights movement within African American communities in the 1940s and early 1950s. The New Deal era played a large part in creating an African American leadership that could take on the white racists in the North and the South. Southern cities such as Atlanta, Georgia, and Birmingham, Alabama, where the African American communities had been established for decades, took the lead in the early days. However, by the 1960s the African Americans who lived in the urban ghettos of the North and West had taken over the fight for equality and civil rights.

A view of storefronts on the 420 block of Lenox Avenue, Harlem, New York City. There is a barber shop, a beauty school, an auto school and a deli. During the 1930s almost 150,000 African Americans settled in Harlem from the southern states.

Free at Last?

5
African Americans in the 1930s

What you will learn

Intermediate 1 and 2
- How the New Deal helped African Americans
- How racism affected the lives of African Americans in the 1930s

Intermediate 2
- Who were prominent African Americans in the 1930s?

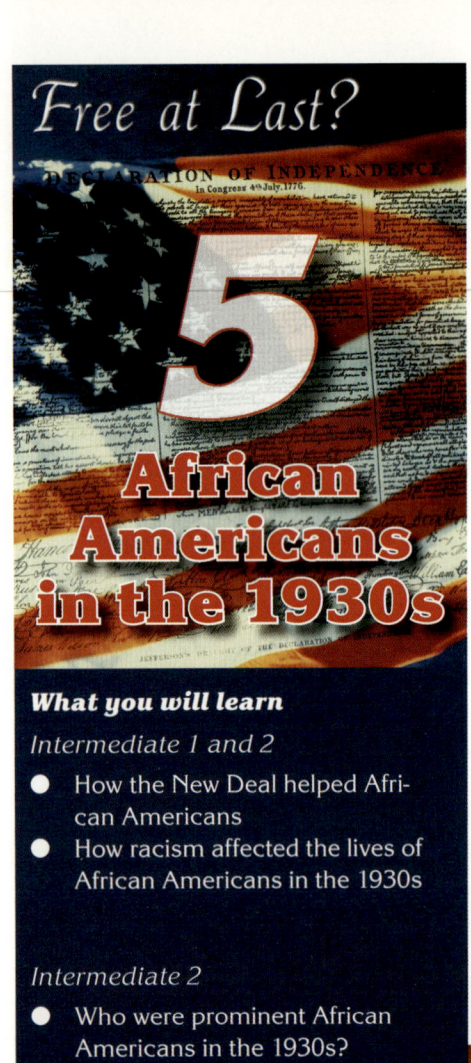

AFRICAN AMERICANS AND THE NEW DEAL

From 1932 President Franklin D Roosevelt and his government attempted to deal with the huge problems of unemployment and poverty created by the Great Depression. One aim of the New Deal was to create jobs for the unemployed and various authorities and organisations were set up to achieve this aim. The Civilian Conservation Corps (CCC) gave jobs to single men aged between 18 and 25. They lived in government camps and worked in the countryside doing hard work such as clearing land, planting trees to prevent soil erosion and helping with flood control. Over three million men took part in the scheme and learned skills which could later help them find proper jobs. One young African American reported from a camp,

"Before we left the bus the officer shouted emphatically, 'Coloured boys fall out in the rear.' The coloured from several buses were herded together, and stood in line until after the white boys had been registered and taken to their tents. We were taken to a permanent camp in the Upper South. There was plenty to eat, and we slept in barracks instead of tents. At the recreation hall we had a radio, piano, a baseball team, boxing squad and classes in various arts and crafts. We worked five days a week, eight hours a day. Our bosses were local men, Southerners, but on the whole, I found nothing to complain of. The work was varied, but it was always healthy, outdoor labour."

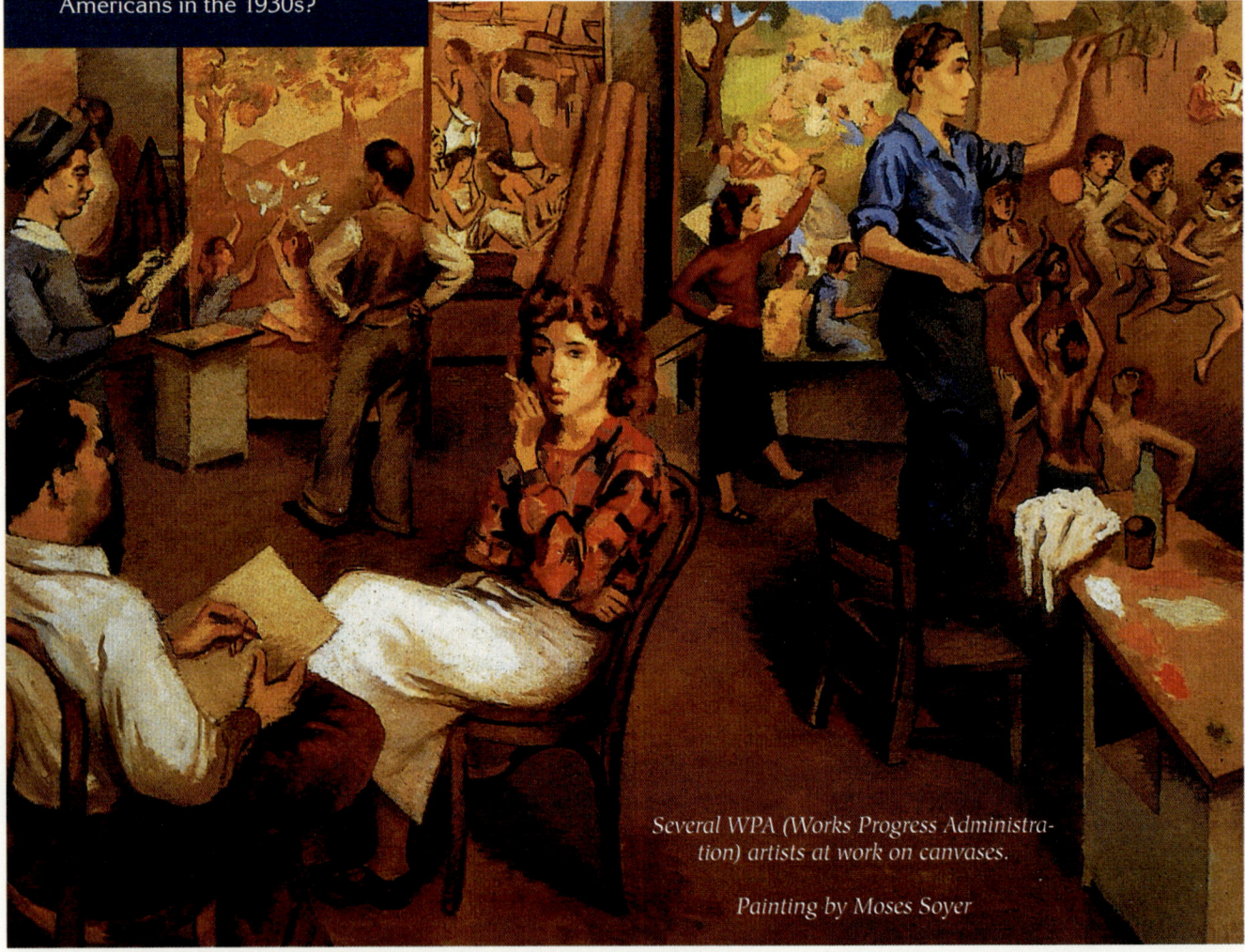

Several WPA (Works Progress Administration) artists at work on canvases.
Painting by Moses Soyer

Job opportunities were provided for African Americans, but there was still plenty of discrimination. In fact for minority groups such as African Americans help was limited by the racist attitudes of the government's civil servants and administrators. For example, minimum wage levels were set at a lower level for African Americans than for Whites.

The *National Industrial Recovery Act* (NIRA) encouraged cooperation between workers and employers. The Act encouraged trade union membership and provided an opportunity for African Americans to become involved in these organisations. More African Americans than ever before joined trade unions in the 1930s. These unions gave African American workers an increased awareness of their civil rights and also increased their confidence in demanding them. NIRA also established the rights of African American workers in law and was therefore an important step towards achieving full civil rights for African American workers.

The Works Progress Administration

A number of New Deal agencies were of some benefit to African American communities. The Works Progress Administration (WPA) employed about one million African Americans in jobs as varied as performing plays and painting murals in post offices. This government agency provided work for unemployed professionals and graduates and encouraged arts projects within different communities. The WPA education programme employed 5,000 African Americans as leaders and supervisors and this led to the WPA teaching 250,000 African Americans how to read and write.

Artists, sculptors, writers and actors were employed by the WPA to take forward a large number of projects. For example, the Federal Writers' Project employed writers to produce guide books and books on local history. In doing this, they carried out oral history projects, gathering information and publishing the memories of those former slaves who were still alive. The WPA sponsored the Federal Theatre Project which enabled 800 African Americans to take part in various theatrical activities, including circus projects, and setting up children's theatres.

Biographical note: Mary McLeod Bethune

The most important African American in President Roosevelt's administration was Mary McLeod Bethune. A friend of the President's wife, Mary was appointed head of the Division of Black Affairs within the National Youth Administration in 1936. She was responsible for the government employing 300,000 African American men and women, or 12% of those African Americans who applied for assistance under the New Deal.

Mary was born in 1875, and she graduated as the only African American student at a Bible Institute in 1895. She set up the Daytona Normal and Industrial Institute for Negro Girls in Florida in 1904. In 1923 her school joined with another African American school in Florida to create the Bethune-Cookman College. In 1935 Mary founded the National Council of Negro Women. Also, she was a director of the National Urban League which was set up to campaign for better conditions for African Americans living in urban areas.

Mary had been an adviser to four US Presidents on issues relating to education and African American affairs when she died in 1955.

The National Recovery Administration

The NRA, set up in 1933, tried to establish job creation schemes and set out rules about working hours and conditions in poorly paid occupations. Many of these schemes were of benefit to immigrant communities and African Americans but for a lot of African Americans the NRA stood for 'Negro Run Around' or 'Negroes Rarely Allowed'.

The *Social Security Act* excluded farmers and domestic workers from participation in this New Deal reform. Therefore, 65% of all African Americans were not eligible for Social Security benefits. US government mortgages were not available to African Americans who bought houses in 'white' areas. Most US government housing programmes built segregated housing. Furthermore, racial discrimination remained a fact of life in most government departments, and in those companies with government contracts.

Despite these problems there was a significant increase in the number of African Americans voting Democrat instead of Republican in the 1936 elections. African Americans were switching their allegiance from the party of Abraham Lincoln and emancipation to Roosevelt in the hope that they would benefit from further New Deal initiatives. President Roosevelt, encouraged by his wife Eleanor, set up an unofficial Federal Council on Negro Affairs or 'Black Cabinet' of educated and influential African Americans to offer him advice. Although it had no real power, it enabled African Americans to press the case for further changes to be made for the social and economic benefit of African Americans. Also, it set the scene for the progress that was to come in the aftermath of the Second World War.

THE SCOTTSBORO BOYS

In 1931 two white girls in Scottsboro, Alabama, accused nine African American youths of raping them on a train travelling between Alabama and Tennessee. The nine youths, aged 13 to 20, were Clarence Norris, Olen Montgomery, Andrew Wright, Willie Robertson, Ozie Powell, Eugene Williams, Charley Weems, Roy Wright, and Haywood Patterson. They became known as the Scottsboro Boys. They were put on trial and found guilty by an all-white jury. The evidence against the boys was chiefly the testimonies of the two girls. Eight of the youths were sentenced to death, and the ninth was sentenced to life imprisonment because he was only thirteen years old.

The case received attention both across the USA and throughout the rest of the world. Many groups and organisations campaigned against what many con-

A poster advertising a defence meeting for Haywood Patterson, one of the Scottsboro Boys, a group of African American youths falsely accused of raping two white girls in Alabama.

sidered to have been an unfair judgement passed on a group of young African Americans by white racists in Alabama. There were appeals against the verdicts and retrials for the next six years before the charges against five of the Scottsboro Boys were dropped. One of the girls admitted that she had been lying when she said that she had been raped. The four remaining young men were given long prison sentences. Patterson escaped from custody. The remaining three Scottsboro Boys who were still in prison were granted parole and eventually set free in 1946. Patterson wrote a book about the case and its aftermath called *Scottsboro Boy* (1950).

The case was seen as one of the most shameful examples of racial injustice in twentieth century America. On the other hand, the Scottsboro Boys were considered fortunate not to have met the fate of so many African Americans accused of rape and other crimes of violence in Alabama, and other southern states. In 1934 when the Scottsboro Boys' appeals were being heard, at least twenty eight African American males were lynched by white racist mobs in the USA. A report on lynchings produced for the Commission on Interracial Co-operation in 1933 said that:

> *"until America can discover and apply means to end these relapses to the law of the jungle, we have no assurance that ordered society will not at any moment be overthrown by the blind passion of an ever-present mob."*

In 1935 Rubin Stacy was a homeless tenant farmer in Florida. Rubin went to the house of a white woman, Marion Jones, to ask for some food. When she saw an African American at her door, Jones was terrified. Stacy was arrested and while being escorted to jail he was taken from police custody by a white mob and lynched. Photographs of Stacy's lynching show a large crowd of white Americans enjoying the event, including many young children.

FACTFILE: Strange Fruit

Abel Meeropol was a white schoolteacher in New York. He was a member of the American Communist Party. In 1937 he saw a photograph of the lynching of two African Americans, Thomas Shipp and Abram Smith. Meeropol said that the photograph "haunted me for days" and this inspired him to write the poem, *Strange Fruit*. He published the poem in the Communist magazine *New Masses* in 1939.

Southern trees bear a strange fruit,
Blood on the leaves and blood at the root,
Black body swinging in the Southern breeze,
Strange fruit hanging from the poplar trees.

Pastoral scene of the gallant South,
The bulging eyes and the twisted mouth,
Scent of magnolia sweet and fresh,
And the sudden smell of burning flesh!

Here is a fruit for the crows to pluck,
For the rain to gather, for the wind to suck,
For the sun to rot, for a tree to drop,
Here is a strange and bitter crop.

Meeropol showed the poem to Billie Holiday who was a famous African American jazz singer. Holiday liked the poem and turned it into the song, Strange Fruit. The record reached number 16 in the music charts in July 1939. However, the song was denounced by *Time* magazine as "a prime piece of musical propaganda" for the National Association for the Advancement of Coloured People (NAACP).

AFRICAN AMERICAN PREACHERS AND MINISTERS

During the 1930s increasing numbers of African Americans attended church. Often churches were the only places where homeless and unemployed African Americans could obtain food, second-hand clothes, and other forms of help. Also, many African American preachers and ministers led campaigns against white racism. In most large cities African American ministers organised boycotts of white shops and other businesses which did not employ African Americans even though they were located in African American areas.

One popular African American preacher was George Baker in Harlem, New York, who was known as the Reverend Major Jealous Divine. He was head of the Peace Mission movement which wanted an end to racism, conflict and hunger. Baker had followers who were white as well as African Americans.

Another popular preacher was Elder Lightfoot Solomon Michaux. He belonged to the Church of God in Washington DC, and he broadcast a daily radio programme that preached the 'happy news' of the gospel. Michaux fed hundreds in his Happy News Café every day, and housed dozens of homeless families in a large building which he had acquired rent-free from a wealthy supporter.

Factfile: The Tuskegee Experiment

In 1932 the US government began a study of the sexually transmitted disease syphilis at Tuskegee in Alabama. The government's white doctors and scientists used poor African American males as their research subjects. Some of these males had syphilis and they were told that they were fortunate to be receiving free treatment from the government. In fact they received no treatment for the disease. Instead the doctors were observing how syphilis affected the men until they died. Details of this study were not published until forty years later, and in 1997 President Clinton made a public apology to the Tuskegee victims and their families.

PROBLEMS IN HARLEM, NEW YORK CITY

Probably the best known and most widely read African American poet of the Harlem Renaissance was Langston Hughes. In 1932 he wrote *Scottsboro Limited: Four Poems and a Play in Verse* to bring attention to the case of the nine youths accused of rape in Alabama. The publication of this work came at a time when Harlem's reputation as the heart of modern African American culture was coming under attack.

During the Great Depression, African Americans faced higher unemployment levels than those facing white Americans. City areas where African Americans lived in large numbers were seen by whites as dangerous places to visit or even travel through. Poverty and crime rather than music, painting and literature were what people thought of when they came across areas like Harlem in New York.

In March 1935 a youth was arrested for stealing a knife in a shop in the centre of Harlem. The youth was held by the shop's security guards until a police officer arrived to question him and take down details of the incident. The police officer took the youth through to the back of the shop, and then let him go through the shop's back door. However, an African American customer thought that the youth had been taken to the basement to be beaten up.

A rumour quickly spread through the streets of Harlem that a white police officer had killed an African American shoplifter. A crowd arrived and looted the shop. As more police arrived a full-scale riot broke out. 250 shops were looted and damaged. Three people were killed, over 100 people were injured, and 125 African Americans were arrested. Harlem's reputation as a centre for African American culture did not recover from this and similar incidents which occurred before and during World War II.

Biographical note: Jesse Owens

James Cleveland Owens was born in Alabama in 1913. He was not a healthy child, suffering from chronic bronchitis and pneumonia. Poor housing and inadequate food and clothing contributed to his poor health. By the age of seven he was picking 100 pounds of cotton a day in the fields where his family worked. When he was nine his family moved to Cleveland, Ohio. When a teacher asked him his name, he answered "JC" which is what he was called by his family. The teacher misunderstood his southern accent and his name was Jesse ("JC") from then on.

At high school, Jesse's sporting abilities became apparent. Many colleges and universities that wanted to have a strong athletics squad tried to recruit Jesse. He decided to attend Ohio State University. However, he was required to live off campus with other African American athletes and when he travelled with the university's sports teams Jesse had to eat at segregated restaurants and sleep in 'blacks-only' hotels. When a 'white' hotel allowed African American athletes to book in, they had to use the back door, and walk up the stairs instead of using the elevator (or lift).

At an athletics meeting in May 1935, Jesse set three world records and equalled a fourth in the space of about 70 minutes. He was selected for the American team for the 1936 Olympics. These games were to be held in Nazi Germany, and Hitler hoped to prove to the world that the Germans were the Master Race. Jesse won the 100 metres, the 200 metres and the long jump, and he was a member of the victorious 4 x 100 metres relay team that won the Gold Medal. In all but one of these events Jesse set new Olympic records and he was the first American to win four gold medals in a single Olympics.

When Owens returned to New York he was granted a ticker tape parade through the city. However, he had to take the freight lift to a reception in his honour at the Waldorf-Astoria Hotel because African Americans were not allowed to use the guests' lifts. Later, Owens said:

"When I came back to my native country, after all the stories about Hitler, I couldn't ride in the front of the bus. I had to go to the back door. I couldn't live where I wanted. I wasn't invited to shake hands with Hitler, but I wasn't invited to the White House to shake hands with the President, either."

Jesse Owens (1913–1980) of the USA at the start of the 200 metres at the 1936 Berlin Olympics which he won in 20.7 seconds, an Olympic record. He won three other gold medals, in the 100 metres, 4 X 100 metres relay and long jump.

When sponsorship and advertising contracts did not come his way, Owens made a living by racing against horses and dogs, and taking part in other publicity stunts. When Owens was criticised for these activities he said:

"People said it was degrading for an Olympic champion to run against a horse, but what was I supposed to do? I had four gold medals, but you can't eat four gold medals."

Owens ran as a professional athlete until 1948, and in a 1950 poll he was voted America's greatest athlete in the first half of the twentieth century, beating the athlete who came second by almost three votes to one. In the 1950s Owens achieved financial security by becoming a public speaker at business conferences, and by setting up a public relations company. In 1976, President Ford presented Owens with the Medal of Freedom, the highest honour the US government can award to a civilian.

Owens died of lung cancer in 1980, but in 1990 President George Bush posthumously awarded Owens the Congressional Medal of Honour. Bush called his victories in Berlin "an unrivalled athletic triumph, but more than that, a triumph for all humanity".

Biographical note: Joe Louis

Joseph Louis Barrow was born in 1914 in Alabama. When Joseph was a baby, his father was committed to the state mental hospital. To help her to feed and look after her children, Joseph's mother remarried although her first husband was still alive. Soon after, the family moved north to Detroit, Michigan.

After working in one of the Ford car factories Joseph became a professional boxer in 1934. He had used the name Joe Louis to keep his boxing career a secret from his mother. Joe gained the nickname the 'Brown Bomber of Detroit'. In 1937 he became world heavyweight boxing champion.

In 1938 Joe Louis fought the German boxer, Schmeling. Although he was not a member of the Nazi Party, Schmeling was seen as a representative of the Nazi regime, and everything Nazism stood for. The African American Louis was seen as the representative of the USA and democracy. Joe Louis was invited to the White House, where President Roosevelt felt the champion's biceps, and said "Joe, we may need muscles like yours to beat Germany."

In front of 70,000 boxing fans at Yankee Stadium in New York, Joe Louis knocked down Schmeling three times in the first two minutes of the first round. The fight was over almost as soon as it began. This was Joe's greatest triumph.

He enlisted in the army in 1942 and fought nearly 100 exhibition bouts against every available opponent to entertain around two million US servicemen. After the war he won four more title fights before retiring as undefeated world heavyweight champion. Joe Louis had earned about $5 million from his fights but his extravagance and generosity left him unable to pay $1.2 million in taxes, penalties and interest demanded by the US government. Forced to return to the boxing ring, Joe Louis lost to his successor as champion, Ezzard Charles, and he retired for good when Rocky Marciano knocked him out in 1951.

Next he became a professional wrestler to pay his debts. After fighting cocaine addiction and other health problems Joe Louis made his living as a host or professional greeter at a casino in Las Vegas. Wealthy gamblers could invite Joe to sit at their table to have their photograph taken with him.

Joe Louis had been a symbol of pride for many African Americans in the 1930s and 1940s due to his skill, sportsmanship and his apparent invincibility when fighting white boxers. In 1981 Joe Louis died in Las Vegas from a heart attack. President Reagan ordered that Joe be buried at Arlington National Cemetery as a national hero.

Biographical note: Paul Robeson

The son of a man who was a runaway slave in his youth, Paul Robeson was born in New Jersey in 1898. He became the best known African American of the 1930s who was prepared to use his reputation to campaign for African American civil rights. He was a university graduate who became an American Football star before turning to acting and singing as his career. In turn he became a successful stage actor, then a singer and recording artist, before becoming a film star in films such as *The Emperor Jones*, *Sanders of the River* and in the musical *Show Boat* when he sang one of the songs that he made famous, *Old Man River*.

Angry at the lack of reform in the USA, he made several trips to the USSR where he made unfavourable comparisons between the hardships facing African Americans in the USA and the lives of ordinary Russians living under the dictatorship of Stalin and the Communists. Robeson said that in the USSR he had felt:

"like a human being for the first time since I grew up. Here I am not a Negro but a human being. Before I came I could hardly believe that such a thing could be. Here, for the first time in my life, I walk in full human dignity."

At the end of World War II Robeson's political activities meant that he was a target for investigation by the anti-Communist House Un-American Activities Committee (HUAC). One witness told the HUAC that anyone who attended Paul Robeson's concerts or who purchased his records was a communist! The HUAC agreed and Robeson and his wife, Eslanda Goode, were declared to be members of the American Communist Party. As Party members Robeson and his wife could not use their passports. Unable to find film or theatre work in the USA and unable to travel abroad, Robeson's annual income dropped from $104,000 in 1947 to $2,000 in 1950.

In 1955 Robeson appeared before the HUAC and denied being a member of the American Communist Party. He said that he supported its policy of being in favour of racial equality. When Gordon Scherer of the HUAC asked Robeson why, if he had felt so free in the USSR, had he not stayed there Robeson replied:

"Because my father was a slave, and my people died to build this country, and I am going to stay here, and have a part just like you."

Robeson suffered from ill health for the rest of his life, but he published his autobiography *Here I Stand* in 1958. He died in Philadelphia in 1976.

THE LINCOLN MEMORIAL

In 1939 the US government asked Marian Anderson to give a concert in Washington DC. Anderson was a successful and popular African American opera singer. However, the Daughters of the American Revolution owned Washington's largest concert hall, the Constitution Hall. The white ladies who represented the Daughters of the American Revolution refused to allow an African American to hold a concert at their venue.

Eleanor Roosevelt, the President's wife, resigned from the Daughters of the American Revolution, and she arranged for Marian Anderson to give her concert on the steps of the Lincoln Memorial in front of a crowd of 70,000 people. The crowd was mostly white, but there were African Americans in the racially mixed audience, in a scene that was similar to the gathering in 1963 when Martin Luther King gave his 'I have a dream' speech at the same site.

The Lincoln Memorial, Washington DC

Free at Last?

6
Changing Times: 1941-1951

What you will learn

Intermediate 1 & 2
- Why the leadership of A Philip Randolph was important for African Americans
- What the 'Double V campaign' was
- Why Executive Order 8802 was important for the civil rights movement
- What the social and economic effects of World War II were for African Americans

Intermediate 2
- Why CORE was set up
- How American attitudes to race and colour began to change between 1945 and 1951

American labour leader A Philip Randolph (1889 - 1979)

THE LEADERSHIP OF A PHILIP RANDOLPH

In 1940, African American protests against racial discrimination grew because African American leaders had failed to persuade President Roosevelt to support their demands for civil rights. The NAACP and the Committee for the Participation of Negroes in National Defence organised protest meetings across the country to demand equal citizenship rights. In January 1941, as the US government increased spending on its defence industries, A Philip Randolph suggested that 10,000 African Americans should march on the nation's capital, Washington DC, insisting that:

"we loyal Americans demand the right to work and fight for our country."

The March on Washington Movement (MOWM)

This represented a more aggressive trend in the African American campaign for civil rights. The MOWM was conceived as an all-African American protest on behalf of ordinary African Americans. The MOWM's agenda included the demand for an order from the President forbidding the awarding of government contracts to firms practising racial discrimination when hiring employees, and a similar order ending segregation and discrimination in the armed forces and in all departments of the US government. Also, the MOWM agenda requested legislation forbidding the benefits of the *National Labour Relations Act* to trade unions that denied membership to African Americans.

AFRICAN AMERICANS AND THE EFFECTS OF WORLD WAR II

Executive Order 8802

However, the March on Washington did not take place. President Roosevelt issued Executive Order 8802 in June 1941. He ordered that there should be no more discrimination in the defence industries because of "race, creed or national origin". However, the MOWM's other aims had not been achieved.

Many African Americans supported the Double-V or Double-Victory campaign during World War II. Because African Americans promised to defend democracy at home and abroad, they hoped that victory in the war against the Nazis in Europe and the Japanese in Asia would be followed by victory against racial discrimination and segregation in the USA. A Philip Randolph said that he wanted to see:

"the stuffing knocked out of white supremacy, and of empire over subject peoples".

More than three million African Americans registered for service in the US armed forces during World War II. More than 700,000 African Americans were serving in the US army by the beginning of 1945. African American servicemen were able to use their heroic service abroad to demand racial justice in the USA.

At the same time, there was an increase in racial tensions as white racist violence against African Americans erupted across the USA. In the summer of 1943 race riots broke out in Los Angeles, Detroit, New York, and in several other American towns and cities as white racists reacted violently against African American demands for full civil rights. In Detroit twenty five African Americans and nine Whites were killed before US troops restored order.

African American membership of trade unions and their employment in offices, as well as in skilled or semi-skilled factory jobs, increased. The heightened expectations of African American veterans returning from war, the growing influence of African American voters, and the continuing migration of African Americans from the South to the North and West, all combined to produce improvements in key areas such as voter registration. Even in the South the number of African Americans registered to vote increased from 200,000 to 600,000 between 1940 and 1946.

AFTER WORLD WAR II

In 1946, the year after World War II ended, Roosevelt's successor, President Harry Truman, set up a Commission on Higher Education which reported that:

"there will be no fundamental correction of the total condition until segregation legislation is repealed".

(continued on page 36)

Biographical note: Asa Philip Randolph

Until the middle of the twentieth century and the development of cheap air travel, most long distance travel in the USA was by railroad. The huge distances between major American cities forced passengers to pay to use sleeping cars (or carriages) provided by the Pullman Company. The Pullman Company employed large numbers of African Americans as porters. These porters carried passengers' luggage, served meals, and were responsible for the comfort of the passengers on these long journeys.

The porters worked long hours, were low paid, and had to rely on passengers' tips to supplement their income. The porters had to pay for their own uniforms and meals, and they were away from home for weeks at a time. In 1925 Asa Philip Randolph founded and became leader of an all-African American trade union with nearly 10,000 members, The Brotherhood of Sleeping Car Porters (BSCP). The Pullman Company refused to recognise this trade union, and would not negotiate with it until 1937. As a result of his hard work and determination, A Philip Randolph won better pay and conditions for sleeping car porters. Also, he became an influential trade union leader, and a leading spokesperson for African Americans.

Biographical note: Dorie Miller

"above and beyond the call of duty"

DORIE MILLER
Received the Navy Cross at Pearl Harbor, May 27, 1942

As one of the African American mess attendants aboard the American battleship USS West Virginia, Dorie Miller served food to the white officers and cleared away their dirty dishes and cutlery. In December 1941, when the Japanese attacked the US naval base at Pearl Harbor, Hawaii, Miller took command of a machine gun on the deck of his battleship. He was responsible for shooting down four Japanese planes. After a campaign by newspapers and civil rights groups, Miller was awarded the Navy Cross, which was the highest award for bravery given to an African American in World War II. Miller was killed in 1943 when the ship on which he was serving as a crew member was torpedoed and sunk by a Japanese submarine.

Factfile: the Tuskegee Airmen

The US Army and Navy remained racially segregated during World War II. However, the US War Department allowed African Americans to be trained as officers, and permitted African Americans to serve as pilots. The 332nd Fighter Group became known as the Tuskegee Airmen because these African American fighter pilots were graduates of the segregated pilot training programme at Tuskegee in Alabama. The Tuskegee Airmen set records for bravery and endurance. Although they made more than 200 flights into enemy territory, this fighter group never lost one of the planes that they were escorting to enemy fighters. The Tuskegee Airmen even sank a German navy destroyer with their gunfire.

Biographical note: Adam Clayton Powell

In 1941, Adam Clayton Powell became the first African American member of New York City Council. His election was chiefly the result of the support he received from the 14,000 members of the Abyssinian Baptist Church where he was the preacher. In 1944 Powell was elected to the US House of Representatives in Washington DC.

At the US Congress Powell was responsible for the desegregation of dining rooms and other facilities which African American congressmen had been forbidden to use. Powell made sure that African American journalists could watch debates in Congress from the press viewing gallery. Because of Powell's hard work, African American students were admitted to the US Naval Academy, and African Americans could be members of the US delegation to the United Nations Organisation.

American pianist and singer Hazel Scott with her husband Congressman Adam Clayton Powell and their son, photographed in London in 1951 where she performed at the London Palladium.

At the same time, Truman used Executive Order 9808 to create the President's Committee on Civil Rights which produced a report called *To Secure These Rights*. This report called for the:

"elimination of segregation, based on race, colour, creed or national origin, from American life".

In response to wartime complaints of African American servicemen who had faced discrimination and segregation in the armed forces, President Truman issued Executive Order 9981 in 1948. This called for:

"equality of opportunity for all persons in the armed forces, without regard to race, colour or national origin".

President Harry Truman set up a Commission on Higher Education.

The Congress of Racial Equality (CORE)

The Congress of Racial Equality (CORE) had been formed in 1942 by James Farmer and members of the Fellowship of Reconciliation (FOR). FOR was an organisation supported by pacifists who opposed war as a means of solving disputes. CORE pioneered the use of non-violent protest as a civil rights strategy, and engaged in its first sit-in in 1943 when Farmer and a group of CORE members employed this tactic against a Chicago restaurant which refused to serve African Americans. In 1947, CORE sponsored a Journey of Reconciliation through some states in the South to test compliance with the Supreme Court decision banning segregation on interstate transportation. This tactic was a forerunner of the Freedom Rides in 1961. In the 1950s and 1960s, CORE concentrated its efforts on voter-registration drives in Southern states.

The Korean War

By the time of the Korean War there was a substantial measure of racial integration in the US armed forces. In 1950, all African Americans in the navy were completely integrated with other servicemen in basic training, technical schools, jobs, and accommodation, while 75% of all African Americans in the air force served in mixed race units. As a result of these developments, in the 1950s and 1960s hundreds of thousands of Americans served in the armed forces, being discharged into civilian life with an experience of racial integration that few Americans had experienced elsewhere.

On the other hand, Truman refused to order government agencies and contractors to employ African Americans during the Korean War, under pressure from Southern Democrats who were opposed to progress on civil rights issues. Truman's efforts to implement a civil rights programme in housing, employment practices, and other areas of everyday life, did not achieve the success of his attack on racial discrimination and segregation in the armed forces.

CHANGING RACIAL ATTITUDES

An example of changing racial attitudes in the USA after World War II was the slow but irreversible integration of African American men and women into cultural activities such as sport. In 1947, the African American baseball player Jackie Robinson left the Negro National League to join the previously whites only Brooklyn Dodgers team in the National Baseball League. Within ten years all major US baseball teams had at least one African American player signed up. However, until 1961 twelve major baseball league clubs segregated their African American and white players when they went to Florida for preseason training.

A portrait of the Brooklyn Dodgers' Jackie Robinson in uniform, preparing to swing a baseball bat.

Free at Last?

7 Education: Separate but equal?

What you will learn

Intermediate 1 & 2
- Why the case of 'Brown v the Topeka Board of Education' was an important step towards African Americans achieving full civil rights
- How 'separate but equal' was declared illegal by the US Supreme Court (1954)

Intermediate 2
- Why the events in Little Rock Arkansas (1957) were important
- Who James Meredith was

In 1863, during the American Civil War, President Abraham Lincoln's Emancipation Proclamation said that the four million slaves in the USA were free people, but most were not set free until Lincoln's army had defeated the rebel Confederates in 1865. As freed slaves, African Americans faced hostility from poor whites who looked upon them as rivals for the few jobs that were available after the Civil War in the defeated rebel states in the South. White racist groups, such as the Ku Klux Klan, were formed to intimidate and terrorise African Americans, and deny them equal opportunities in the South.

Freed slaves had full US citizenship as a result of the 14th Amendment to the Constitution, and as citizens they were entitled to vote. In the South, African Americans were denied the right to vote by literacy tests and other methods designed to prevent poor and often illiterate ex-slaves and their descendants from voting.

SEPARATE BUT EQUAL

A 'separate but equal' policy which allowed US states to provide racially segregated schools, hospitals and other facilities was made possible in 1896. In that year the US Supreme Court said that segregation based on race was legal so long as separate but equal facilities were provided for each race. That ruling remained in force until 1954 when the Supreme Court outlawed segregation in schools. In 1956, when Rosa Parks and other African Americans refused to travel on segregated buses in Montgomery, Alabama, they started a campaign of direct action against the laws that denied African Americans their full civil rights by forcing them to use separate facilities.

African American protests against racial segregation in public places helped African Americans in the USA to regain their civil

The Ku Klux Klan intimidated and terrorised African Americans and denied them equal opportunities in the South.

Segregation was the way of life in the southern states of America. Here four African American males sit on the left hand side of the cinema. Whites would sit on the right hand side of the barrier.

rights. Restaurants and other public places were soon desegregated. In the 1960s, President John F Kennedy insisted that young African Americans should be taught in desegregated schools, colleges and universities. Kennedy's successor, President Lyndon B Johnson, supported new laws aimed at restoring full civil rights to African Americans, including the right to vote in state and federal elections.

BROWN V THE TOPEKA BOARD OF EDUCATION

In the small town of Topeka in the state of Kansas, the NAACP helped the father of Linda Brown take his local Board of Education to court over the separate but equal facilities in local schools. The case of an eight-year-old African American girl, and her father's desire that she attend the best school available whether or not it was supposed to be for whites only, reached the US Supreme Court.

On 17 May 1954, the US Supreme Court said that it was illegal for local school boards to segregate their schools according to the pupils' race. The Supreme Court said that the separate educational facilities provided by the Board of Education were not equal, so they should be desegregated as soon as possible. The judges had decided to reverse the decision taken by the US Supreme Court in 1896 that made it legal for school boards to provide separate but supposedly equal facilities for African American and white children.

Petitions

In the summer of 1955, representatives of the NAACP organisation in the southern states of the USA met in Atlanta, Georgia. Among those African American leaders in attendance was Medgar Evers who supervised NAACP activities in Mississippi. (Evers was shot and killed at his home by a racist gunman in June 1963. His assassin, Byron de la Beckwith, was not found guilty of his murder until 1994.) These NAACP leaders drafted a standard petition that African American communities could submit to their local school board, after they had gathered the signatures of as many people as possible. The petition asked that each local school board comply with the judgement of the US Supreme Court and desegregate its schools. The petition reminded school boards that they were:

"duty bound to take immediate concrete steps leading to the early elimination of segregation in the public schools."

The usual response from school boards to these petitions was rejection. At the same time, the names and addresses of those who had signed the petition were published in local newspapers, inviting threats and intimidation from white racists.

Most states in the South tried to ignore the Supreme Court's decision to end school segregation. One school board district in Texas and two in Arkansas were desegregated, but in the

39

National Guardsmen standing outside Little Rock Central High School and a large group of white students standing with them to prevent any African American students from entering, during the first year of the desegregation of public schools in Arkansas.

rest of the South not one school was desegregated in 1954. White politicians and government officials in the South decided to wait until they received specific instructions on how to end school segregation in their school board districts before they did anything.

Little Rock Arkansas (1957)

In September 1957, nine African American teenagers tried to become students at the whites-only Central High School in Little Rock, Arkansas. Their names were MinniJjean Brown, Elizabeth Eckford, Ernest Green, Thelma Mothershed, Melba Patillo, Gloria Ray, Terrance Roberts, Jefferson Thomas and Carlotta Walls. The State Governor of Arkansas called on the National Guard to prevent the African American students from entering the school, while a crowd of hostile white adults and teenagers threatened the nine African American students and their supporters.

Daisy Bates, who was president of the NAACP in Arkansas, encouraged the nine students to meet at her house before they were taken to Central High School each day. At various times Bates's

40

house was stoned, shot at and bombed, and Ku Klux Klan members set up burning crosses in her front garden. Racists forced businesses not to put adverts in the newspaper owned by Bates and her husband, the *Arkansas State Press*. As a result, the newspaper was forced to close down, with the Bates family losing their main source of income.

On the first day that the nine African American students were able to enter the High School, the local police made no attempt to prevent a crowd of racists from rushing into the school. The nine students were forced to escape in a car. Later, MinniJean Brown was suspended from the school when she poured chilli over the head of a male student who was calling her racist names in the school's dining hall. As the oldest member of the group, Ernest Green was the first and only one of the Little Rock Nine to graduate from the High School with a diploma. In June 1958, Martin Luther King attended the graduation ceremony, where he sat beside Green's mother and Daisy Bates. Instead of the applause that greeted the names of the white students, there was silence when Green's name was called out. However, Green said:

> *"I figured they didn't have to, because after I got that diploma that was it. I had accomplished what I had come here for."*

The bravery of these African American students in the face of white racist hostility had shown that states would find it very difficult to ignore the US Supreme Court's decision to end school segregation in future.

JAMES MEREDITH AND THE MISSISSIPPI LAW SCHOOL

James Meredith surrounded by newsmen after enrolling at the University of Mississippi in 1962

James Meredith had served in the US Air Force for nine years. In 1960 he returned to his home in the state of Mississippi and applied to become a student at the whites-only University of Mississippi. With his application forms, Meredith enclosed a note which told the university that he was an African American. The university sent Meredith a telegram telling him that his application was too late to be considered for entry in 1960.

Meredith took the University of Mississippi to court, accusing it of rejecting his application because he was an African American. The NAACP paid for Meredith's legal costs, and in September 1962 the US Supreme Court ruled that he should be allowed to become a student at the university. Then President Kennedy issued an order that Meredith's entry to the University of Mississippi should not be blocked for any reason. At the same time Kennedy issued an executive order telling the US Secretary of Defence to take any steps which were needed to make sure that Meredith could attend the university.

On 30 September 1962, a crowd of white racists attacked the University of Mississippi's administration building. The mob believed that Meredith was inside the building. Several hundred policemen, who were armed with only tear gas and clubs, were no match for the white mob who attacked with guns and firebombs. A French journalist and a local man were killed, and 160 policemen were injured. The next day US troops arrived, and James Meredith was escorted under guard to register as a student at the university's law school. Meredith was accompanied to his classes and lectures by armed guards, and at one time 20,000 US troops were stationed in and around the university grounds. In August 1963 James Meredith graduated from the law school.

Free at Last?

8 The Montgomery Bus Boycott

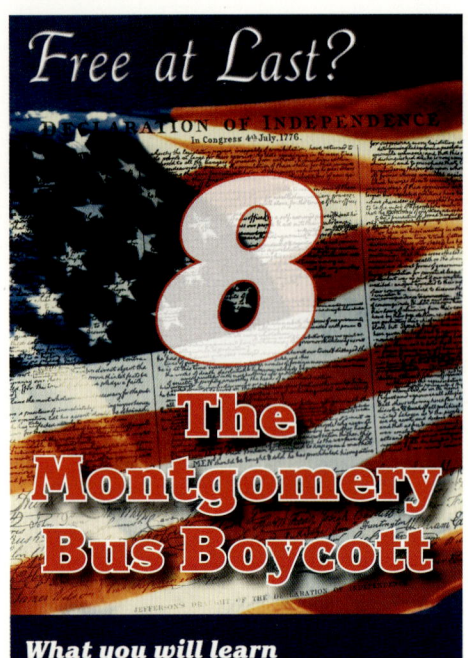

What you will learn

Intermediate 1 & 2
- Why African Americans refused to use the buses in Montgomery, Alabama
- How Martin Luther King became an important leader of the civil rights movement
- What happened during the Montgomery Bus Boycott

Intermediate 2
- Why Martin Luther King Junior believed in non-violent resistance to racist violence.

Mrs Jo Ann Gibson Robinson was president of the Women's Political Council (WPC), a local African American women's organisation in Montgomery, Alabama. In 1953, the WPC complained to the City Commission in Montgomery about the treatment of African American passengers on the city's buses. In particular, African Americans complained about the bus company's confusing seating policy that varied from route to route, and from driver to driver.

African American passengers were expected to shift their seats when ordered to do so by white drivers, and to give up their seats to white passengers. Also, African American passengers had to get on the bus at the front door, pay their fare to the driver, get off the bus to board at the back door, and then find a seat. Sometimes the drivers would drive off before the African American passengers had been able to get back on the bus at the back door. This happened at a time when most bus passengers in Montgomery were African Americans, taking at least 30,000 journeys every day, and paying the City Lines bus company about $20,000 in fares each week.

In 1954, Mrs Robinson wrote to the Mayor of Montgomery, W A Gayle, demanding better conditions for African American passengers on the city's buses. Robinson threatened to organise a boycott of the city's buses by African Americans if significant improvements were not made. This would mean that African Americans, who represented nearly three-quarters of the bus company's regular passengers, would refuse to travel on racially segregated buses under the existing arrangements.

Biographical note: Mrs Rosa Parks

As a result of the part she had played in the Montgomery Bus Boycott, Rosa Parks became famous throughout the USA, and was a heroine for African Americans. In 1957 she left Montgomery and moved to Detroit, Michigan. She was employed as an administrative assistant by John Conyers who was a politician and a member of the US Congress. Mrs Parks received many awards and honorary degrees in recognition of the important work she had done for the African American community and the civil rights movement. In 1987 she founded the Rosa and Raymond Parks Institute of Self-Development. This was a training centre for young African Americans. In 1999 she was awarded the Congressional Gold Medal for her act of defiance which led to the Montgomery Bus Boycott. The photograph opposite shows her being escorted by the US House Speaker Dennis Hastert while President Clinton watches in the background.

MRS ROSA PARKS

Mrs Rosa Parks was 43, an African American, and she was employed as a seamstress in the Montgomery Fair department store in the centre of Montgomery, Alabama. She was well educated, and belonged to the local branch of the NAACP. Like many African Americans, Mrs Parks had been put off buses in Montgomery on several occasions for refusing to obey Alabama's segregationist laws. At 5.30 pm on Thursday 1 December, Mrs Parks had got on the bus at Dexter Avenue close to the shop where she worked. A few minutes later a group of white men got on the bus at the Empire Theatre stop. Mrs Parks refused to obey the bus driver's order to give up her seat to a white man. She was arrested, charged with breaking the city's segregation laws, and fined $14.

The next day, Mrs Jo Ann Gibson Robinson produced over 35,000 leaflets to be distributed throughout Montgomery to the city's 40,000 African American inhabitants. (See above.)

Meanwhile, Edgar D Nixon, a leading member of the NAACP in Montgomery, visited Mrs Parks and told her that the African American community could end segregation on public transport by using her arrest as a reason for organising a bus boycott by African Americans in the city. Since the authorities had charged Mrs Parks with breaking Alabama's state law on segregated seating on all public transport, she could appeal all the way to the United States Supreme Court in Washington DC. She could challenge the right of Alabama's politicians to segregate seats on public transport in that state.

> *Another Negro woman has been arrested and thrown in jail because she refused to get up out of her seat on the bus for a white person to sit down ... If we do not do something to stop these arrests, they will continue. The next time it may be you, or your daughter, or mother ... We are therefore asking every Negro to stay off the buses on Monday in protest at the arrest and trial. Don't ride the buses to work, to town, to school or to anywhere on Monday ... Please stay off all buses on Monday.*

The leaflet used to encourage African Americans to boycott Montgomery's buses.

Six days earlier, the Interstate Commerce Commission had banned segregation on all vehicles and in all facilities engaged in interstate transportation (including buses). Alabama's law ignored the Commission's ban on segregation on all forms of public transport. Mrs Parks said to Nixon:

"You know, Mr Nixon, if you say so, I'll go along with it."

Next, a group of twenty African American church leaders, under the direction of Nixon, formed the Montgomery Improvement Association (MIA), to organise and coordinate what became a one-year boycott of the city's buses by African Americans.

MARTIN LUTHER KING'S LEADERSHIP OF THE MIA

Martin Luther King and his young wife Coretta had moved to Montgomery from Atlanta in 1954. He was elected as president of the MIA chiefly because Edgar D Nixon refused to run for the presidency. Nixon knew that his work as leader of an African American trade union would take him away from Montgomery on a regular basis, and that the MIA president needed to be in the city most of the time. Also, as a newcomer to the city of Montgomery, King had made fewer enemies than the other main candidate for the MIA presidency, the Rev. L Roy Bennett.

King was surprised at his election, since he had steered clear of local politics and civil rights campaigns during his year in Montgomery. In fact he had never met Mrs Parks before his election to the leadership of the MIA. However, as a result of his actions during the Montgomery Bus Boycott, King became an important leader of the civil rights movement in the USA.

In 1953, African Americans in Baton Rouge, Louisiana, had boycotted that city's buses, forcing an agreement which said that passengers would be given first come/ first served segregated seating. Refusing to cooperate with the racists who ran the buses had shown that African Americans could use their economic power as passengers to bring about change.

Biographical note: Martin Luther King Jr.

Martin Luther King Junior (his father was known as Martin Luther King Senior) was born in Atlanta, Georgia, in 1929. Like his father, Martin Junior became a minister and when Rosa Parks was arrested, he was in charge of the Dexter Avenue Baptist Church in Montgomery. As a result of the Montgomery Bus Boycott Martin Luther King (we will leave out Junior from now on) became involved in the civil rights movement. He took part in many marches and demonstrations. His speeches and written works inspired other civil rights leaders, and he became an African American leader who was famous throughout the world.

At the age of 39, King was murdered in Memphis, Tennessee, in April 1968. He left a widow and four young children as well as many heartbroken followers.

In 1955, the MIA in Alabama only asked for greater courtesy towards African American passengers from bus drivers; the hiring of African American drivers on predominantly African American routes; the seating of African Americans from the back towards the front, and Whites from the front to the back, without sections always being kept clear for either race. When white politicians in Montgomery refused to discuss these points, the MIA decided to demand the elimination of racial segregation on the buses.

THE BUS BOYCOTT

The MIA decided to extend the boycott indefinitely. In the end, the bus company's services were boycotted by 99% of Montgomery's African Americans for over a year. The African American women who were employed as domestic servants in Montgomery's whites-only areas made the greatest sacrifice during the boycott. For more than a year, these low paid women walked long distances to and from work in support of the bus boycott.

White community leaders in Montgomery tried to force the MIA leadership and the African American community into abandoning the bus boycott. When better off African Americans organised car pools to give other African Americans lifts to and from work, the police stopped the cars and accused the drivers of committing a large number of minor offences.

Next, Whites put pressure on local insurance companies to cancel the policies of African American car owners who were helping the MIA by supporting its car pools. MIA leaders received anonymous threatening phone calls, and were accused of breaking Alabama's anti-boycott law. Martin Luther King was arrested for an alleged speeding offence, and was jailed for the first time in his life. On 30 January 1956, King's house was firebombed and badly damaged by white racists.

Victory?
The bus boycott ended on 21 December 1956 after the US Supreme Court announced that Alabama's bus segregation laws were illegal. However, most other facilities and services in Montgomery remained segregated for many years to come. Montgomery's city council decided to close the city's parks rather than allow African Americans to use them. In 1965, Martin Luther King returned to Montgomery to complain about the slow pace of desegregation in that city and in the rest of Alabama.

Martin Luther King's Non-violent Principles

Mohandas K Gandhi had led millions of Indians in their struggle against British rule over India until it became an independent state in 1947. He believed that his supporters should not obey the unfair laws of the British, and that they should be willing to go to prison for breaking or disobeying those laws. At the same time Gandhi insisted that his followers should never use violence against their British opponents. He said that his followers should try to win the sympathy of their enemies by non-violent resistance to their unfair laws. Gandhi used the term "satyagraha", which means "hold us to the truth" in English, to encourage his followers not to fight back when attacked or provoked by their British opponents. Gandhi hoped that his followers' bravery would touch the hearts of their enemies, and change British attitudes towards the Indian people's struggle for freedom.

Throughout the bus boycott King urged the African American community in Montgomery not to retaliate or to be provoked into violence by white racists. As someone who had studied the non-violent campaigns of Gandhi against British rule over India, King did not want the bus boycott to become an excuse for violent conflict between African Americans and white racists. He said:

Gandhi

"We are not advocating violence. We want to love our enemies. Be good to them. Love them and let them know you love them. I want it to be known that ... if I am stopped, our work will not stop. For what we are doing is right, what we are doing is just."

Non-violent resistance demanded commitment, courage and discipline. As a result of the bus boycott a group of African Americans calling themselves the Fellowship of Reconciliation printed a pamphlet called *Martin Luther King and the Montgomery Story*. This pamphlet was distributed to thousands of African Americans who wanted to learn how to take part in non-violent resistance. A young minister called James Lawson helped Martin Luther King to run workshops to teach African Americans and their white supporters how to use this tactic against white racists. At these workshops the learners had to be prepared to sit quietly while their friends and colleagues pretended to be racists and shouted at them, pushed them and even spat at them.

Not all African Americans believed that non-violent resistance would defeat white racism. Many African Americans refused to take any insults, and were determined to fight back against white racists.

Free at Last?

9

The Southern Christian Leadership Conference

What you will learn
Intermediate 1 & 2

- Why the Civil Rights Act (1957) was an important step towards achieving civil rights for African Americans
- Why the SCLC was set up
- What sit-ins achieved and the part played by the SNCC in this campaign
- Why the freedom riders set out across the USA

THE CIVIL RIGHTS ACT (1957)

The *Civil Rights Act* of 1957 disappointed civil rights campaigners. Lyndon Johnson, who was the leader of the Democrats in the US Senate, had persuaded Democrats from the South to support a civil rights law so weak that it would not lead to an increase in the number of African American voters in the South. The rest of the Democrats were happy to support a law that was the first civil rights law passed by the US federal government for eighty two years. Over the next twenty years further civil rights legislation would be introduced by the US government.

President Eisenhower's Republicans were unhappy to see that there would be no increase in the number of African Americans who were registered to vote in the South. African American voting rights was one area where the Republican Party was on the same side as the civil rights activists since more African American voters in the South would weaken the power of the Democrats in that area. African Americans in the South who could vote tended to vote Republican. Martin Luther King admitted to having voted for the Republicans in 1956.

THE SCLC

In 1957, Martin Luther King and African American religious leaders from ten states in the American South formed the Southern Christian Leadership Conference (SCLC) to encourage and coordinate non-violent civil rights protests in the South. The SCLC did not have individual members, since it did not want to be seen as a rival organisation to the NAACP. Instead, the Southern Baptist ministers who made up most of the SCLC portrayed King as a leader of national importance, and tried to

A student sit-in at a cafeteria in Arkansas

support African American boycotts in other cities, similar to the successful Montgomery Bus Boycott.

When subsequent boycotts met with little success, the SCLC focused its efforts on African American voting rights, and embarked on an unsuccessful three year campaign to double the number of African Americans registered to vote in the South. Its lack of financial resources and poor organisation meant that the SCLC had achieved little by 1960.

SIT-INS AND THE SNCC

In February 1960, four African American students from North Carolina Agriculture and Technical College ordered coffee in their local Woolworth's store in Greensboro. As all seats in the restaurant were reserved for whites only, the students were refused service. The four students remained seated until the store closed that evening. The next day, the students returned with some friends and continued their non-violent protests against racial segregation in public places.

Ella Baker had been the SCLC's temporary executive director, but she had little belief in Martin Luther King's leadership abilities. In fact she believed that King showed too little respect for the key role that women had played in the civil rights movement since World War II. In April 1960, Baker organised a meeting of student leaders in Raleigh, North Carolina.

As a result of this meeting, the Student Non-violent Coordinating Committee (SNCC) was established. Baker was aware that

FACTFILE: Freedom Schools

Up until the early 1960s many African American children in the South worked on their parents' farms rather than attend school on a regular basis. School attendance was not compulsory as it had been in Britain since the nineteenth century.

A civil rights project was set up in 1964 called 'Freedom Summer'. This project led to Freedom Schools being opened to teach reading, writing and maths to African American children in some Southern states. Also, community centres were set up to provide legal and medical services to poor African Americans.

Some of these Freedom Schools were called Citizenship Schools. At these schools African American students were taught how to stand up for their civil rights as well as learning how to read and write. They were taught about the US Constitution, and how democracy was supposed to mean equal treatment for all people in the USA. They were encouraged to believe that it was important for African Americans to vote in elections. However, in the South many African Americans could not vote because they had to pass a literacy test before their names could be added to the list of voters. Therefore, the Freedom Schools taught thousands of African Americans how to pass the literacy test by teaching them how to read and write.

FREEDOM RIDES

On 5 December 1960, the case of 'Boyton versus the State of Virginia' led the US Supreme Court to declare that racial segregation in interstate bus stations and terminals was illegal. The next year the Freedom Rides began. CORE (Congress of Racial Equality) sponsored thirteen African American Freedom Riders to travel on buses between states to find out if bus stations were being desegregated. they did this by attempting to use whites-only toilets and waiting rooms.

The Freedom Riders' bus journeys all began in Washington DC, and they planned to travel throughout the South until their scheduled arrival in New Orleans on 17 May 1961. On 14 May Freedom Riders on one bus were attacked in Birmingham, Alabama. One of the Freedom Riders was paralysed for life.

President Kennedy stepped in to protect the protesters with police escorts, but he urged African Americans to focus on voter registration projects as a safer and less provocative form of civil rights activity. Meantime, the Interstate Commerce Commission acted to order the desegregation of interstate bus stations and terminals. In 1962 CORE organised the Freedom Highways campaign to encourage companies and private owners to desegregate hotels, motels and restaurants along interstate routes and highways.

young African American students, and their white friends, were growing increasingly dissatisfied with the leadership offered by King and the SCLC. She encouraged the SNCC to retain its own identity which was separate and distinct from the SCLC, or any other African American organisations.

The use of the sit-in tactic to protest against racial segregation spread across the USA. By October 1960 sit-ins had taken place in 112 cities in the South. Student protesters sat in segregated bus stations, restaurants, waiting rooms and any other public places where African Americans were denied service, or were treated as inferior to Whites.

These non-violent direct action protests included wade-ins at segregated swimming pools and beaches, stand-ins at segregated theatres and cinemas, and pray-ins at segregated churches. The response of Whites was mixed. Many companies, including all of the Woolworth stores, desegregated their restaurants, while some local authorities closed down public facilities rather than desegregate them.

48

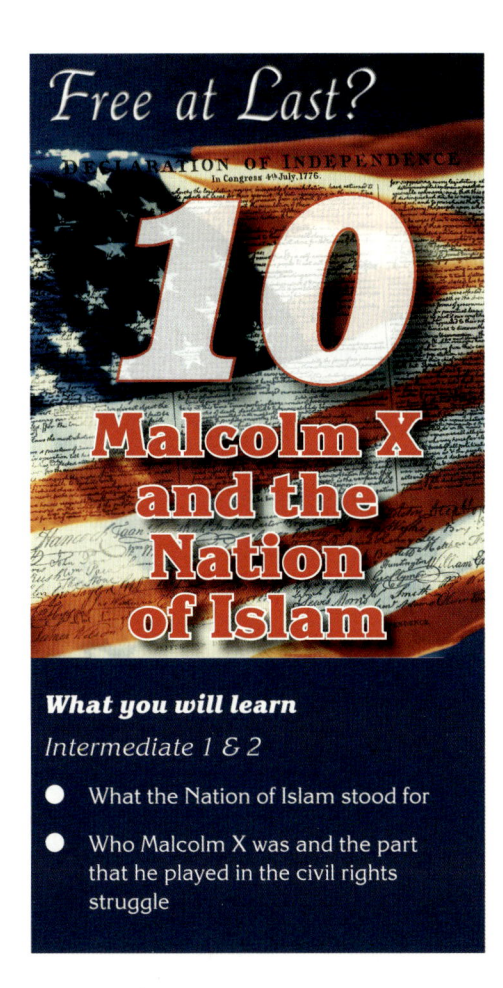

Free at Last?

10 Malcolm X and the Nation of Islam

What you will learn

Intermediate 1 & 2

- What the Nation of Islam stood for
- Who Malcolm X was and the part that he played in the civil rights struggle

THE NATION OF ISLAM

Some African Americans who rejected the non-violence of the civil rights campaigns in the 1950s were attracted to the Nation of Islam and its support for African American separatism rather than integration. The Nation of Islam said that African Americans had to establish themselves as a separate Islamic nation within the USA.

The Nation of Islam was founded in Detroit, Michigan, by Wallace D Fard in 1929. This movement was based on the Moorish Science Temple founded in 1913 by the Prophet Drew Ali. Fard disappeared without trace in 1934. Elijah Poole, who was leader of the Nation of Islam's Chicago mosque, took control of the movement. Adopting the name of Elijah Muhammad, the new leader moved the Nation of Islam's headquarters to Chicago, Illinois. Elijah Muhammad's message was that African Americans should be proud of their African heritage, and that white Americans were devils and therefore evil.

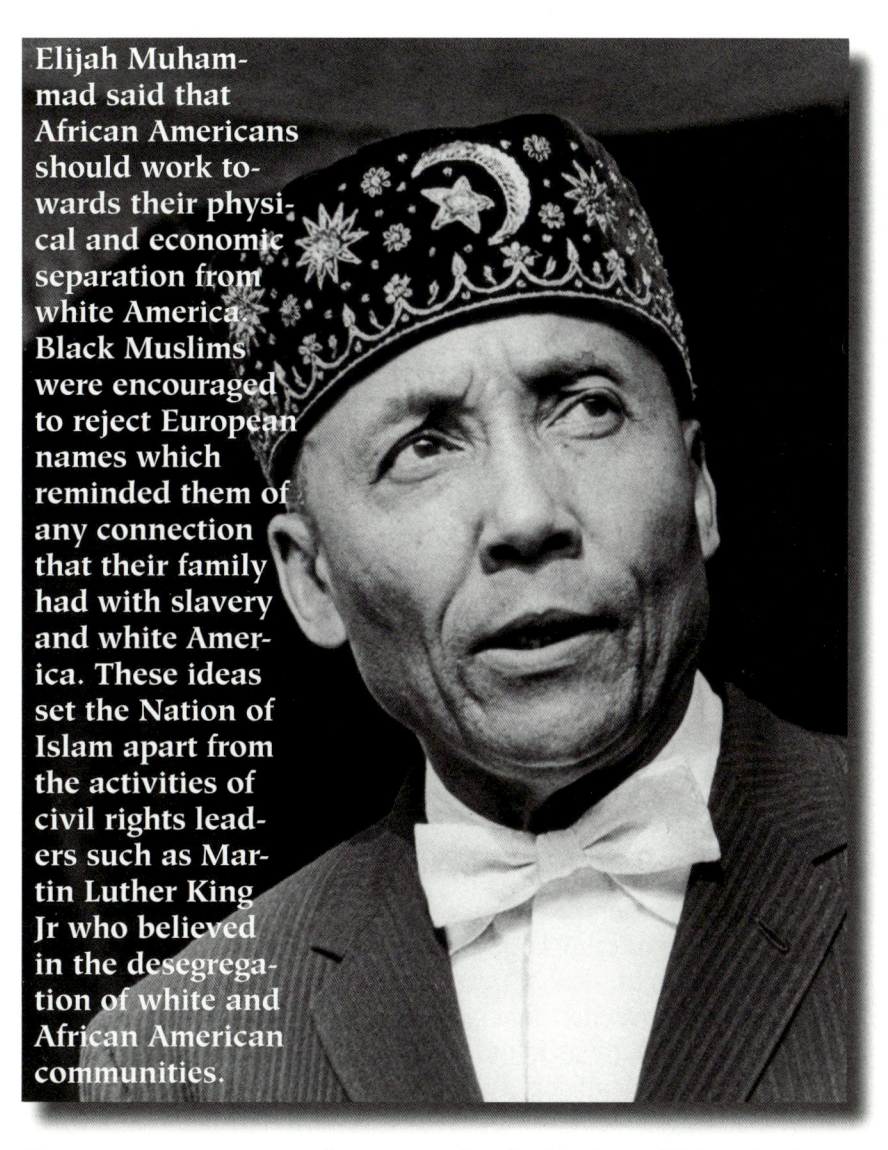

Elijah Muhammad said that African Americans should work towards their physical and economic separation from white America. Black Muslims were encouraged to reject European names which reminded them of any connection that their family had with slavery and white America. These ideas set the Nation of Islam apart from the activities of civil rights leaders such as Martin Luther King Jr who believed in the desegregation of white and African American communities.

The most important spokesperson for the Nation of Islam in the late 1950s and early 1960s was Malcolm Little, or Malcolm X as he called himself when he rejected his European or 'slave' name.

Biographical note: Malcolm X

Malcolm Little was born in Omaha, Nebraska, in 1925. He was the son of an African American Baptist minister, and a West Indian mother. He was the fourth of their eight children. His father, Earl Little, was a supporter of Marcus Garvey's UNIA (Universal Negro Improvement Association). Following threats from the Ku Klux Klan, the Little family moved to Lansing, Michigan.

When Malcolm was six his father was attacked by white racists who belonged to the Black Legion, and he was thrown to his death under the wheels of a tramcar. His mother suffered a breakdown and was admitted to a mental hospital.

When Malcolm left school in 1941 he went to live with an older half-sister in Boston, Massachusetts. He became involved with criminals, and moved to New York when the USA became involved in World War Two. In 1945 Malcolm returned to Boston and was sentenced to seven years in prison for burglary. In prison Malcolm discovered that his brothers Philbert and Reginald and his sister Hilda had joined the Nation of Islam. When he was released from prison in 1952 Malcolm was made a member of the Nation of Islam by Elijah Muhammad, and took the Black Muslim name of Malcolm X. Soon he became one of the movement's most effective speakers.

MALCOLM X JOINS THE NATION OF ISLAM

In 1954, soon after he was released from prison, Malcolm X became the principal minister of the Nation of Islam's Temple Number 7 in Harlem, New York. Soon he began to draw large crowds and a great deal of publicity with his speeches attacking the racism that was found throughout American society.

As a spokesperson for an organisation that combined elements of a religious movement and a political party, Malcolm X aimed his message at the African Americans who lived in the slums of America's large cities, and who thought that they had little to gain from the peaceful campaigns for civil rights by groups such as the Southern Christian Leadership Conference (SCLC).

In the 1960s, Malcolm X became dissatisfied with the slow progress being made by the Nation of Islam in attracting African Americans to the movement. He realised that a large number of African Americans thought that many of the religious beliefs of the Black Muslims were difficult to accept, and that the majority of African Americans believed that racial separation was not likely to be achieved. So Malcolm X attracted increasing attention and support from urban African Americans for his speeches attacking both white racism and the non-violent beliefs of so many civil rights leaders.

Since Elijah Muhammad discouraged Black Muslims from participating in civil rights protests, Malcolm's speeches focused on the social and economic issues facing so many

African Americans living in America's cities. He highlighted problems such as slum housing, high rents, poorly resourced schools, and African Americans' lack of political influence at local and national levels.

Malcolm X said:

> *"I am black first ... My sympathies are black, my allegiance is black, my whole objectives are black ... I am not interested in being an American, because America has never been interested in me."*

Rejecting the peaceful strategies of King and the other civil rights leaders, Malcolm X said that African Americans had to resist white racism by any means necessary. He said that there were two types of African American. There were the Uncle Toms who wanted a peaceful life, and were willing to live beside white Americans (he took this name from the African American slave hero of the famous antislavery novel written by a white author, *Uncle Tom's Cabin*). Martin Luther King was accused by Malcolm X of being an Uncle Tom. Malcolm X said that:

> *"You don't have to criticise Reverend Martin Luther King. His actions criticise him. Any Negro who teaches other Negroes to turn the other cheek is disarming the Negro ... of his God-given right ... his moral right ... his natural right to defend himself. Everything in nature can defend itself except the American Negro."*

Malcolm X said that the other type of African American was the New Negro. New Negroes such as the Black Muslims were proud of their race, colour and culture. They demanded total racial separation, not desegregation.

MALCOLM X LEAVES THE NATION OF ISLAM

When President Kennedy was assassinated in November 1963, Elijah Muhammad ordered Black Muslims not to comment on this political crisis. Malcolm X made some comments on the assassination and Elijah Muhammad suspended him from speaking as a Black Muslim minister for three months. In March 1964, Malcolm X resigned from the Nation of Islam and announced that he was going to set up his own temple in New York, to be known as Muslim Mosque Incorporated. The MMI would support racial separation, but it would adopt a more direct approach to tackling issues facing all African Americans, whether or not they had adopted Islam.

Next, Malcolm X left the USA to tour Middle Eastern and African states, as well as making a pilgrimage to Mecca as a Black Muslim. Meeting Islamic pilgrims of all races and colours in Mecca persuaded him to break away from Elijah Muhammad's Nation of Islam. Malcolm X converted to the Islamic faith, taking the name El-Hajj-Malik El-Shabazz.

On his return to the USA, Malcolm X, as he continued to be known, set up the Organisation of Afro-American Unity (OAAU). The OAAU was:

> *"dedicated to the unification of all people of African descent in this hemisphere and to the utilisation of that unity to bring into being the organisational structure that will project the black people's contribution to the world."*

The death of Malcolm X

The OAAU had fewer than 1,000 members when Malcolm X was shot and killed. On 21 February 1965, he was speaking at a rally of supporters in New York City when three assassins fired revolvers and a sawn-off shotgun at him, killing him almost instantly. His killers were alleged to have been connected to the Nation of Islam.

The *Autobiography of Malcolm X*, as told by Malcolm to the author Alex Haley, had been published in 1964. It was a best-seller, and in 1992 the African American film director Spike Lee made *Malcolm X*, a feature film largely based on the book. This film brought the life and times of Malcolm X to the attention of a new generation of young Americans.

Biographical note: Muhammed Ali

Cassius Clay was born in 1942. He became a hero for many African Americans when he won the light-heavyweight boxing gold medal at the 1960 Olympic Games in Rome. When he was only 22 years old he became the heavyweight champion of the world by beating the champion Sonny Liston in seven rounds. Clay successfully defended his world title against the former champion Liston, and another former champion called Floyd Patterson. Clay was very light on his feet for a heavyweight boxer, and he boasted that he could "float like a butterfly and sting like a bee". Often he accurately predicted in which round he would win a fight. Within a few years Clay had become one of the most famous sportsmen in the world, and a spokesperson for African Americans at the height of the civil rights campaign.

In 1964 he joined the Nation of Islam, abandoning his 'slave name' Cassius Clay and adopting the name Muhammed Ali. When selected for military service in 1967 Ali refused to fight in the Vietnam War. As a Black Muslim he claimed that he was a conscientious objector who would not fight in a white man's war against non-white Asians. Ali was charged and found guilty of draft evasion. He was sentenced to five years in prison. Furthermore, the boxing authorities in the USA stripped Ali of his world title, and banned him from fighting at the peak of his boxing career. Many Whites and some African Americans accused him of being a coward and a traitor.

Freed on appeal against his conviction, Ali had to wait three years for the US Supreme Court to throw out the charges against him. He was able to return to boxing. In 1971 he fought for the heavyweight championship of the world against the new champion Joe Frazier in what was called the 'Fight of the Century'. Ali was defeated by the younger, fitter champion. In 1973 Ali defeated Frazier and won the right to fight the new champion, George Foreman, in Zaire. Foreman was thought to be unbeatable, but in the fight known as the 'Rumble in the Jungle' Ali defied all the odds and knocked out Foreman in the eighth round. Then he won a third fight with Frazier in 'The Thriller in Manila'. He lost his title to Leon Spinks, but regained it by beating Spinks, becoming the first man to win the world heavyweight title three times.

Ali retired in 1979, but he returned to challenge Larry Holmes for the world heavyweight title, when he suffered the only knockout in his long boxing career. After he retired in 1981 his life was marked by ill health and increasing infirmity. Most experts blamed Ali's health problems on the physical punishment he had received during his long boxing career.

Free at Last?

11

Birmingham, Alabama

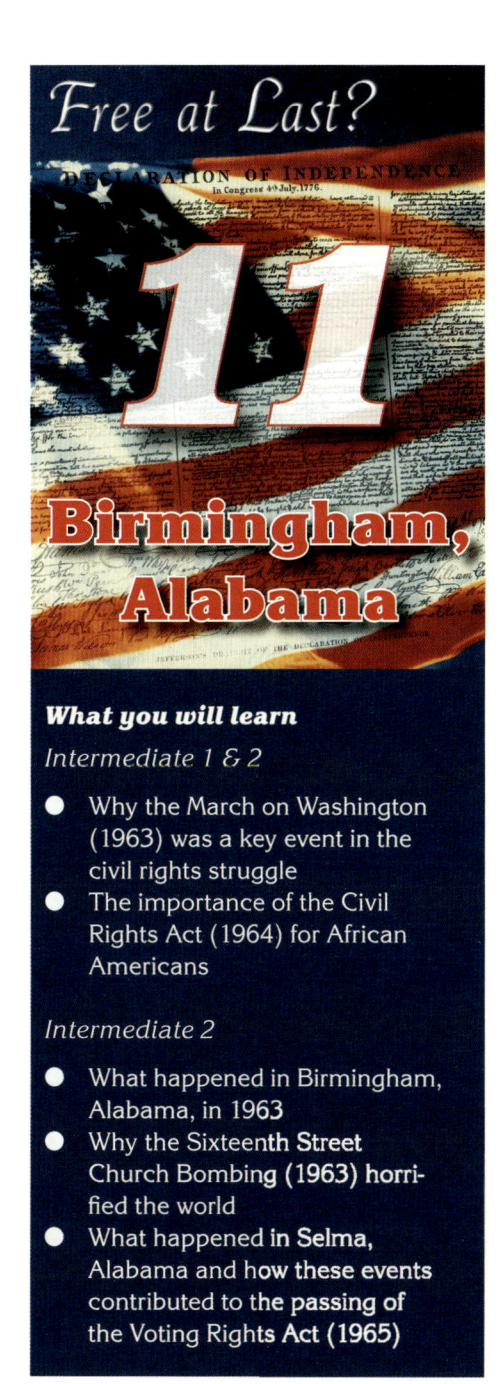

What you will learn

Intermediate 1 & 2

- Why the March on Washington (1963) was a key event in the civil rights struggle
- The importance of the Civil Rights Act (1964) for African Americans

Intermediate 2

- What happened in Birmingham, Alabama, in 1963
- Why the Sixteenth Street Church Bombing (1963) horrified the world
- What happened in Selma, Alabama and how these events contributed to the passing of the Voting Rights Act (1965)

BIRMINGHAM, ALABAMA (1963)

Sit-in protests, Freedom Rides and other protests against racial segregation provoked violent acts of retaliation from white racists in many American towns and cities. In April 1963, William Lewis Moore decided to deliver a letter to the Governor of Mississippi demanding an end to racial hatred and intolerance. Moore was a white postman from Baltimore, and as he walked from his home in Maryland to Mississippi, he was shot and killed by white racists in Alabama on 23 April.

Birmingham, Alabama, was the most important industrial city in the South. It was a city where most public facilities remained rigidly segregated. Martin Luther King accepted an invitation from Birmingham's civil rights organisation to lead a campaign against shops and other businesses in the city which refused to desegregate their restaurants, changing rooms, toilets and drinking water fountains.

The campaign also planned to target businesses that either would not hire African Americans, or would not promote them to positions of responsibility. King hoped to remain in Birmingham long enough to persuade the city's white leaders to work with African American leaders to draw up a timetable for desegregating all aspects of city life.

Martin Luther King's letter from Birmingham Jail

The two leaders of the Birmingham campaign were Martin Luther King and the Rev. Fred Shuttlesworth. Before the campaign began both men were arrested. In Birmingham jail, King wrote a long letter to those members of the civil rights movement who thought that he should back off to avoid any trouble in Birmingham.

Their critics said that King and Shuttlesworth should trust white supporters to force white politicians to introduce more civil rights reforms. King wrote that he believed that white moderates who did not take direct action against the prejudice and discrimination facing African Americans were a bigger obstacle to civil rights than members of the Ku Klux Klan.

"I must make two honest confessions to you, my Christian and Jewish brothers. First, I must confess that over the last few years I have been gravely disappointed with the white moderate. I have almost reached the regrettable conclusion that the Negro's great stumbling block is not the White Citizen's Counciler or the Ku Klux Klanner, but the white moderate who is more devoted to 'order' than to justice; who prefers a negative peace which is the absence of tension to a positive peace which is the presence of justice; who constantly says 'I agree with you in the goal you seek, but I can't agree with your methods of direct action'; who paternalistically believes that he can set the timetable for another man's freedom."

Martin Luther King salutes the crowd at the March on Washington

THE VIOLENCE BEGINS

On 2 May 1963, Eugene 'Bull' Connor, the white racist Commissioner of Police in Birmingham ordered the arrest of over 900 young people aged 6 to 18 who attempted to join a civil rights march. The next day, Connor used dogs and high-pressure water hoses to frighten and intimidate the civil rights demonstrators who continued to object to the city's segregation rules.

On the third day, the firemen's hoses were not turned on, but hundreds of civil rights marchers were arrested.

At this stage, some African American leaders wanted to call off the protests, as they were worried that someone could be killed if the demonstrations continued. At the same time, aware that the violent events of the previous couple of days had been broadcast on television across America, local businessmen wanted a peaceful end to the situation. Good publicity for the civil rights movement was bad for business in the city of Birmingham. Local businesses were prepared to compromise, and offered to desegregate waiting rooms, changing rooms, and other facilities within ninety days.

Next, the motel which was the demonstrators' headquarters and the place where many of the civil rights activists were living was firebombed by white racists. As they ran out of the building, the civil rights activists were attacked by policemen ordered to the scene by the State Governor of Alabama. A riot broke out as the protesters fought back. Many people were injured, and several buildings were burned down.

THE MARCH ON WASHINGTON (1963)

Two African American leaders, A Philip Randolph and Bayard Rustin organised a March on Washington for civil rights on 28 August 1963. More than thirty Freedom Trains, and 2,000 Freedom Buses were hired to transport marchers to the capital city from all over the USA. More than 200,000 marchers assembled in front of the Lincoln Memorial in the capital city of the USA.

Most of the marchers were African Americans, but about 20% of the crowd was made up of white marchers who were demonstrating their support for the civil rights movement. The demonstration was peaceful and orderly, and millions of people across America watched on television as Martin Luther King gave his 'I have dream' speech to the assembled crowd.

In his famous speech, King said:

"I have a dream that one day on the red hills of Georgia the sons of former slaves and the sons of former slave holders will be able to sit down together at the table of brotherhood. I have a dream that one day even the state of Mississippi … will be transformed into an oasis of freedom and justice … I have a dream that one day the state of Alabama … will be transformed into a situation where little black boys and black girls will be able to join hands with little white boys and white girls and walk together as sisters and brothers."

However, not all civil rights campaigners were prepared to share King's dream. One African American civil rights activist said:

"I sat there thinking that in Canton (Mississippi) we never had time to sleep, much less dream."

The Sixteenth Street Church Bombing (1963)

On 15 September 1963, white racists bombed the Sixteenth Street Baptist Church in Birmingham, Alabama, killing four young African American girls called Addie Mae Collins, Denise McNair, Carole Robertson and Cynthia Wesley. Three of the girls were fourteen, and the youngest was eleven. This horrific event took place at 10.25 am on a Sunday morning, and Bible class had just ended when the bomb exploded.

Fourteen others were injured in the bomb blast, and groups of African Americans took to the streets to protest at this horrific attack on a place of worship. White racists who were involved in the plot to bomb the church were not identified and charged with the crime until more than thirty five years later.

Later on the day of the bombing, local policemen were ordered to fire shots over the heads of the protesters to disperse them. One sixteen-year-old African American boy was killed by a policeman's shotgun blast in the back. Another African American boy, thirteen-year-old Virgil Lamar Ware, was riding through Birmingham on the handlebars of his brother's bike when he was shot at and fatally wounded by a member of a group of white teenagers who were on their way back from a demonstration in support of segregation.

THE CIVIL RIGHTS ACT (1964)

The protests and other activities of the Congress of Racial Equality (CORE) and the Student Non-violent Coordinating Committee (SNCC) forced the American President, John F Kennedy, to send federal marshals from outside each of the states involved to protect protesters from racist policemen, and force universities to desegregate their facilities for students.

The *Civil Rights Act* (1964) banned racial segregation in public areas, and racial discrimination in education and employment. Nevertheless, in many states where there was a history of racial tension, white racists made sure that few African Americans could vote. This was despite the 15th Amendment to the US Constitution stating that the right to vote should not be denied on account of a person's race or colour.

When African Americans had attempted to register to vote, literacy tests and other obstacles that did not apply to white voters were used to prevent them from voting. When a few African Americans had succeeded in registering to vote, they became targets for Whites who belonged to the Ku Klux Klan, as well as being intimidated and threatened by racist employers and local sheriffs and police officers who did not want African Americans to exercise their right to vote.

Dr Martin Luther King (centre) leading civil rights marchers on the last leg of their fifty mile Selma to Montgomery march in Alabama on 25 March 1965.

SELMA, ALABAMA

In 1964 three civil rights campaigners who were trying to organise the registration of African American voters in Mississippi were murdered by white racists. In protest the Mississippi Freedom Democratic Party tried to prevent an all-white Mississippi delegation from representing that state at the national convention of the Democratic Party. This protest was not successful, but when national television broadcast the civil rights campaigners' demonstrations this brought the issue of racism in politics to public attention across the USA.

Jimmie Lee Jackson was an activist who encouraged other African Americans to register to vote. On 26 February 1965, Jackson was murdered in Alabama. Mr Jackson was beaten and shot by local policemen as he tried to protect his mother and grandfather from a racist attack on civil rights marchers. Martin Luther King and other African American leaders organised a protest march from Selma, Alabama, to Montgomery, that state's capital.

When the marchers tried to cross the Edmund Pettus Bridge on the outskirts of Selma, they were attacked by policemen on horseback. On national television, viewers saw the unarmed demonstrators being beaten and tear-gassed. Two days later, the marchers' second attempt to cross the bridge was abandoned when state troopers blocked the way. President Johnson ordered Alabama's National Guard to protect the 300 protesters allowing the march to be completed on 25 March 1965. This time the marchers were accompanied by 50,000 supporters from many different races.

The Rev. James Reeb was one of several white clergymen who joined the Selma to Montgomery march after the marchers had been attacked at the Edmund Pettus Bridge. Reeb was beaten to death by white men who attacked him as he walked down a Selma street on 11 March. Mrs Viola Gregg Liuzzo was a white woman from Detroit who saw the television broadcasts of the attacks on the marchers. She drove alone to Alabama to support the civil rights marchers. Mrs Liuzzo was shot and killed

A group of voters lining up outside the polling station in Peachtree, Alabama, a year after the Voting Rights Act was passed

by Ku Klux Klansmen as she drove some civil rights marchers back to Selma on 25 March 1965.

The Voting Rights Act (1965)

A few weeks later, the US Congress passed the *Voting Rights Act*, a law banning literacy tests and other obstacles to African Americans being able to register to vote. Any areas which wanted to change election procedures, possibly to make life difficult for African American voters, had to obtain permission from the US Justice Department. At the same time, the US Attorney General could send federal examiners to register African American voters in areas where the US government believed that the local registrars were not registering enough African American voters.

Federal examiners were sent to Virginia, North Carolina, South Carolina, Georgia, Florida, Tennessee, Mississippi, Alabama, Louisiana, Missouri, Arkansas and Texas between 1965 and 1967. In 1967 alone, the Attorney General sent examiners to sixty two counties in Alabama, Mississippi and Louisiana to register African American voters in rural areas where they made up a majority of the population.

The long-term result of the *Voting Rights Act* was that increasingly African Americans could use their votes to force politicians to pay more attention to the needs of the African American community. Within five years of the Act being passed, 60% of African Americans had registered to vote in the American South, compared to only 20% being registered to vote in 1960. In the state of Mississippi the number of African American voters increased from 7% in 1964 to 59% in 1968. In the 1970s, African American mayors were elected in large Southern cities such as Atlanta and New Orleans.

Free at Last?

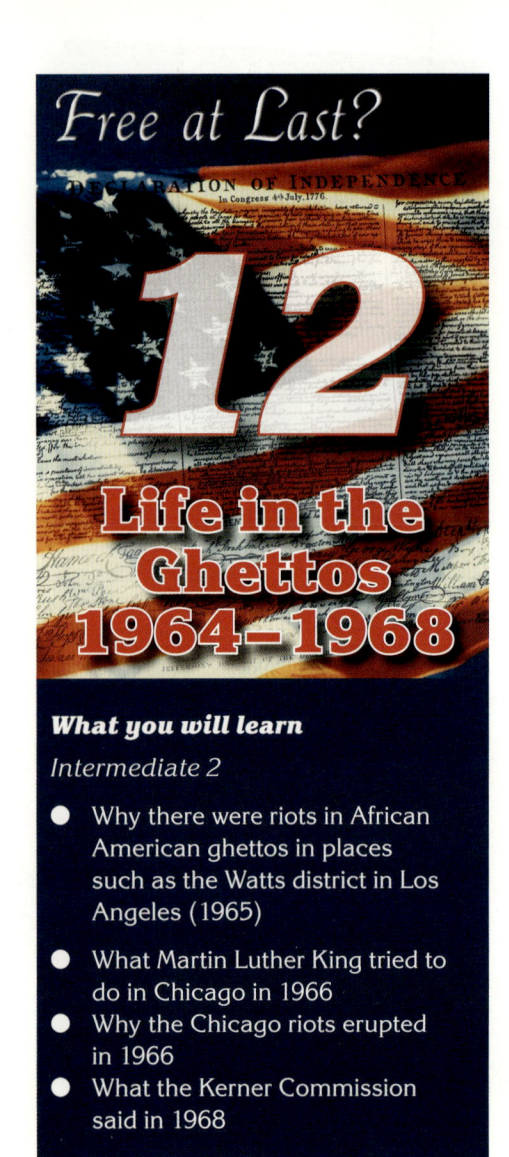

12

Life in the Ghettos 1964–1968

What you will learn

Intermediate 2

- Why there were riots in African American ghettos in places such as the Watts district in Los Angeles (1965)
- What Martin Luther King tried to do in Chicago in 1966
- Why the Chicago riots erupted in 1966
- What the Kerner Commission said in 1968

By the mid-1960s the main aims of the civil rights campaigners in the South had been achieved through their non-violent protests, and their refusal to retaliate in the face of racist violence and intimidation. Support from local and state governments in the South for segregation and discrimination had been defeated by the intervention of Presidents and the federal government in support of the civil rights campaigners.

However, the civil rights campaigns had not tackled the problems facing African Americans outside the South—in the cities of the North, and the West. During the 1960s, about half of all African Americans had moved from the South and lived in cities. These African Americans knew that they faced segregation and discrimination almost as bad as anything they or their parents and grandparents had faced in the South.

The movement of African Americans from the rural South to the cities of the North and West, combined with the movement of better off Whites from the inner cities to the suburbs, had created African American urban ghettos. The inhabitants of these slum areas or ghettos suffered from the effects of poverty, high unemployment, a lack of health services, low educational standards, overcrowded housing, high crime rates, and police intimidation and brutality.

Slums in Washington DC where African Americans lived in the shadow of the Congress building

RIOTS

Between 1964 and 1968 many African Americans rejected the non-violence of the Southern-based civil rights movement. In the spring and summer months of every year from 1964 to 1968 there were riots in the African American ghettos of almost every major American city. These riots were often sparked off by acts or even rumours of police brutality.

The most serious riots were in New York (1964), the Watts area of Los Angeles (1965), Newark in New Jersey (1967) and Detroit, Michigan (1967). The assassination of Martin Luther King in April 1968 led to riots in 125 American cities, with shootings, arson and looting in and around the African American ghettos. During these riots buildings were set on fire and burned down, hundreds of people were injured or killed, thousands of African Americans were arrested, and many areas or neighbourhoods were burnt out and abandoned by their inhabitants.

The Watts Riots (1965)

On 11 August 1965 a white policeman called Lee Minikus stopped and arrested a young African American driver called Marquette Frye for drunk driving and speeding in the Watts district of Los Angeles. A crowd gathered, police reinforcements arrived, and trouble broke out. Complaints about police racism and brutality were common among the 250,000 people who lived in the Watts district where 98% of the inhabitants were African Americans.

Two days later there were riots that led to arson, looting and a series of shooting incidents. Fourteen thousand troops from the US National Guard and several thousand police officers took six days to restore order to the Watts district. The Watts riots caused $45 million damage to private property. Thirty four people were killed, and nine hundred people were injured. Four thousand African Americans were arrested, and hundreds of families were made homeless.

An African American storekeeper stands outside his shop, which has a sign reading, 'This store is owned and operated by Negroes,' during the race riots in Newark, New Jersey 14 July 1967. There is writing scrawled on the window, reading 'Soul Brother'.

MARTIN LUTHER KING AND CHICAGO (1966)

Mayor Richard Daley of Chicago had tried to make sure that there would be no rioting in Chicago's ghetto neighbourhoods where 800,000 African Americans lived. Daley provided money to ghetto districts in order to fund youth centres, nurseries and a Foster Grandparents programme. Daley's use of the city's anti-poverty funds to benefit African Americans was aimed at winning their support for his methods of running Chicago. However, most of Chicago's African Americans lived below or close to the poverty line and despite representing nearly one-third of the city's population they played little or no part in running their own communities.

In January 1966, Martin Luther King decided to move to one of the slums on Chicago's West Side and bring public attention to the problems facing those who lived in ghetto housing. King rented an apartment for his family in a ghetto neighbourhood called North Lawndale. Shortly before the King family moved in, the landlord sent four plasterers, two painters, and two electricians to renovate the property before the world-famous civil rights campaigner moved into what was known locally as 'Slumdale'. Despite the repairs King was able to show newspaper reporters that his family was living in what could only be described as a slum.

Over the next few months, King met local African American gang members, spoke at several public meetings, and organised a rent strike in a tenement slum. Mayor Daley organised an expensive publicity campaign to discredit King's attempt to highlight the problems facing Chicago's African Americans. Public sympathy for King's rent strike fell away when it was discovered that the landlord who owned the slum where the rent strike was taking place was very old, seriously ill, and almost as poor as his tenants who were not paying their rents.

Mayor Daley of Chicago

The Chicago Riot (1966)

In late June 1966, when Chicago police officers turned off a water hydrant that had been turned on by some youths in a ghetto neighbourhood on a hot day, a riot began. African Americans in Chicago had little respect for police officers in a city where 250,000 African Americans had

Ronald Everett (Maulana Karenga)

The Watts riots and their aftermath had a profound effect on Ronald Everett. He was from Los Angeles, and he was president of the African American student body at his junior college. He urged African Americans to discover their cultural and historical roots in Africa. He adopted the name Maulana Karenga, and he developed the rituals of Kwanzaa which became a popular winter festival celebrating the African heritage of the USA's African Americans. Later he admitted that Kwanzaa had not been celebrated in Africa or anywhere else before 1966.

Kwanzaa — A Celebration of Family, Community and Culture

"I said it was African because you know black people in this country wouldn't celebrate Kwanzaa if they knew it was American. Also, I put it around Christmas because I knew that's when a lot of people would be partying."

been stopped and searched by the local police in 1965.

The mayor's police force had developed elaborate anti-riot tactics which included flying squads of police officers who could be sent to deal with any incidents as soon as they were reported. Nevertheless, four thousand police officers were needed to bring five thousand rioters under control. Two people were killed, hundreds were injured, and four hundred African Americans were arrested.

At the end of August 1966, Mayor Daley met with King and other African American leaders in Chicago. Daley promised to set up a Leadership Council for Metropolitan Open Housing to bring to an end housing discrimination against African Americans wishing to move out of the slums. Critics of the agreement noted that it contained no timetable for ending housing discrimination because of householders' race and colour. Also, few African Americans in Chicago could afford to move, even when they wanted to leave the slums.

However, Daley's promise to do something to improve slum housing in Chicago allowed King and his family to claim a victory on behalf of those who lived in the ghettos, and to leave their slum apartment in 'Slumdale'. The King family returned as quickly as possible to their home in Atlanta, Georgia.

That summer, across the USA, there were thirty eight riots in African American ghettos. These riots led to seven deaths, four hundred injuries, three thousand arrests and $5 million worth of damaged property. The Chicago riot showed that Martin Luther King had little or no influence over the actions of the inhabitants of the urban ghettos. King's support for non-violent protest, and his willingness to make agreements with white politicians, was out of step with the attitudes of those young African Americans who were rioting across the USA.

In the long hot summers a fire hydrant was used to cool down in the ghettos. In Chicago this led to a riot in 1966 when police tried to intervene.

THE KERNER COMMISSION

President Johnson ordered an official investigation (the Kerner Commission) into the urban riots in the African American ghettos. In 1968 when the Kerner Commission reported, it said that 40% of African Americans were living in poverty. The Commission showed that African American unemployment levels were nearly double those of whites, and the report concluded that the riots and high crime rates in African American ghettos were caused by the effects of poverty.

Sounds of the Ghetto: Rhythm and Blues, Motown and Soul

The Four Tops were a very successful group.

In the 1950s, Rhythm and Blues music developed out of earlier African American music styles such as Blues, Gospel, Jazz and Swing. This new style of music appealed to young African Americans and some young Whites. Chuck Berry was a Rhythm and Blues musician who wrote songs about teenage life, with many of his compositions such as *Roll Over Beethoven* and *Johnny B. Goode* being sung and recorded by white Rock 'n' Roll musicians. Other Rhythm and Blues artists who were very popular in the 1950s were Ray Charles, Fats Domino and Bo Didley.

Rhythm and Blues music was first produced in the South, in cities such as New Orleans, Louisiana, and Memphis, Tennessee. Then, as increasing numbers of African Americans moved north and west to escape from the poverty and racism of the South, musicians played and recorded their music in cities such as New York, Chicago and Detroit. Berry Gordy set up the Motown Record Company in 1958. Originally based in Detroit, the Motor Town, Gordy's Motown company produced recordings that blended elements of white Rock 'n' Roll with African American Gospel and Rhythm and Blues. He experimented with recording techniques in his studios, and he hired the most talented musicians and songwriters to produce recordings that would appeal to all Americans.

African American singers and musicians who were recorded by Motown included Diana Ross and the Supremes, Gladys Knight and the Pips, the Four Tops, the Temptations, the Jackson Five, Stevie Wonder and Smokey Robinson. In the South, Soul music developed out of Blues, Gospel and Rhythm and Blues. Popular Soul singers included James Brown, the 'Godfather of Soul', Aretha Franklin, the 'Queen of Soul', as well as Otis Redding, Al Green and Curtis Mayfield. At the height of the civil rights struggle, these performers were seen as positive role models for young African Americans.

To this day many of these singers from the 1950s, 1960s and 1970s tour, record and appear on television throughout the world. At the same time African American music has continued to develop and it remains popular with people of all ages, races and cultures. Rhythm and Blues, Motown and Soul evolved into the many forms of music produced by young African Americans today.

Free at Last?

13

Black Power

What you will learn
Intermediate 1 & 2

- Who Stokely Carmichael was and why he spoke about 'Black Power'
- The part the Black Panthers played in the civil rights struggle

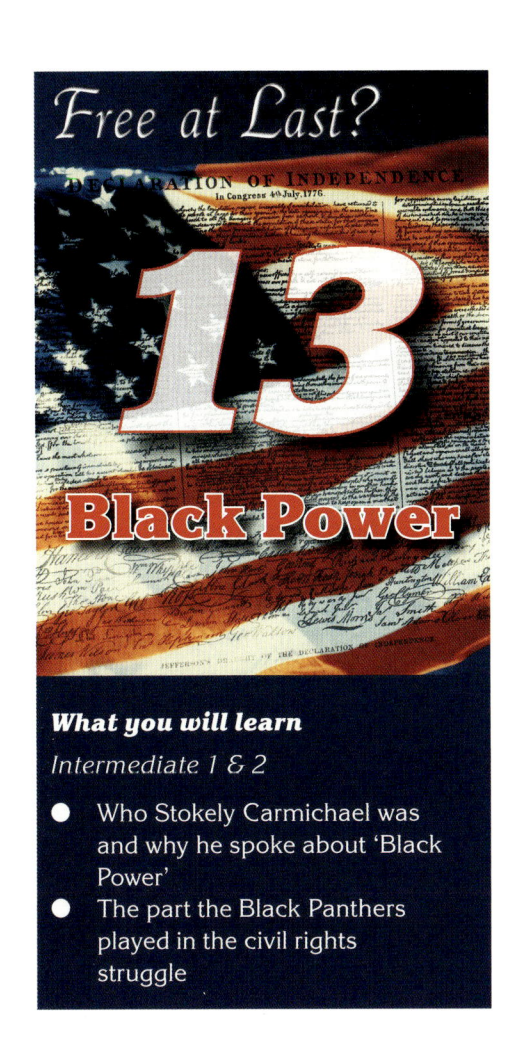

In June 1966, James Meredith planned a 220 mile solo protest March Against Fear through rural Mississippi. He wanted to show African Americans that they should not allow fear of white racist violence to prevent them from exercising their civil rights or asserting their right to vote. James Meredith had been the young African American who had campaigned successfully to be allowed to enter the all-white University of Mississippi in 1962.

Meredith received many death threats before he began his march, but he set out from Memphis, Tennessee on 5 June. The next day, as he crossed the state boundary from Tennessee into Mississippi, he was shot in the back, neck, head and legs by sixty birdshot pellets fired by a member of the Ku Klux Klan.

In hospital, Meredith said that he regretted not carrying a gun when he set off on his March Against Fear. When it was pointed out that his attitude was not in keeping with the principles of non-violent protest, James Meredith said:

> *"Who the hell ever said that I was non-violent? I spent eight years in the military and the rest of my life in Mississippi!"*

SOUTHERN RACISTS FIGHT BACK

When the new *Civil Rights Act* was passed by the US Congress in 1964, there was a frightening increase in racist violence against African Americans in the South. Because President Johnson and members of the Democratic Party in the North

Biographical note: James Meredith

James Meredith was born on 25 June 1933 in the state of Mississippi. He served in the US Air Force from 1951 to 1960. As a civilian he attended Jackson State College for two years before becoming the first African American student at the University of Mississippi in 1962. His arrival at the University led to riots and the deaths of two people.

In 1966 Meredith decided to carry out his March Against Fear. This was a solo march from Memphis, Tennessee to Jackson, Mississippi, which was supposed to show that African Americans in rural Mississippi need not fear physical violence when exercising their civil rights, such as walking to a polling station to vote. Meredith was shot and badly injured on the second day of his march. Martin Luther King and other leading civil rights leaders decided to complete Meredith's march on his behalf.

In 1972 Meredith stood as a candidate but failed to be elected to the US Congress. In 1989 he decided to work for the conservative US Senator, Jesse Helms.

and West supported desegregation, white Democrats in the South left the party in their thousands. At the same time, Republican politicians who admitted to holding racist views began to enjoy considerable success in local and national elections in the South. White politicians in the South who remained Democrats also gave their backing to racist opposition to desegregation and the other aims of the civil rights movement.

One racist politician who gained a great deal of support for his open hostility to African American civil rights was George Wallace, several times governor of Alabama. As racist politicians such as Wallace became spokespeople for white racist opposition to African American civil rights, some SNCC and CORE activists realised that campaigns for voting rights and desegregation were not going to succeed unless violence against African Americans was stopped. When neither President Johnson nor the US Congress tried to end racist violence, important members of the SNCC and CORE began to consider renouncing their commitment to non-violent protest.

STOKELY CARMICHAEL AND BLACK POWER

African American anger at the racist attacks which usually resulted from peaceful civil rights protests forced some civil rights activists to consider abandoning non-violent protest. Stokely Carmichael was a member of the SNCC in Alabama who had decided to join other civil rights activists from across the USA to complete Meredith's March Against Fear through Mississippi. On 16 June Carmichael was arrested by the police at a civil rights rally in a place called Greenwood. When he was released from jail there was a crowd of several thousand African Americans waiting to cheer him. Carmichael announced to the crowd:

> *"This is the twenty seventh time I have been arrested, and I ain't going to jail no more! The only way we gonna stop them white men whuppin' us is to take over. We been saying freedom for six years, and we ain't got nothin'. What we gonna start saying now is Black Power!"*

The Black Power slogan and a clenched fist symbol were adopted by CORE. The slogan and symbol were used by young African American activists who were no longer willing to take beatings at the hands of white racists. To these young African Americans the slogan repre-

(continued on page 66)

Biographical note: Huey Newton

Huey Newton was born in 1942. His father named his son after the Southern racist politician Huey Long from Louisiana. His father was an active member of the NAACP who believed that Long's policies brought benefits to the African American community. For instance, he believed that segregation created jobs for African Americans which would have been taken by better educated Whites if there had been no separate facilities for the different races.

As a student in Oakland, California, Newton met Bobby Seale. In 1966 they set up the Black Panther Party. In 1968 Newton was found guilty of voluntary manslaughter. When he was released from prison Newton turned his back on political violence. He became involved in community work such as helping the homeless, but in 1974 he was arrested and charged with murder and assault with a deadly weapon. Freed on bail, Newton escaped to Cuba. In 1977 he returned to the USA, and after two juries failed to reach a decision on the earlier charges, he became a free man.

Newton became a student at the University of California. In 1980 he was awarded a PhD in social philosophy. He was shot dead in 1989.

Stokely Carmichael was born in Trinidad, in the West Indies, in 1941. In 1952, Carmichael moved to the United States to live with his parents who had left him with his grandmother until they had established themselves in their adopted country. He attended high school in New York City. As a student at Howard University, and a member of the SNCC, Carmichael became one of the Freedom Riders in 1961.

In an interview for *Life* magazine in 1967, Carmichael explained why he had become a Freedom Rider. He said:

"When I first heard about the Negroes sitting in at lunch counters down South, I thought they were just a bunch of publicity hounds. But one night when I saw those young kids on TV, getting back up on the lunch counter stools after being knocked off them, sugar in their eyes, ketchup in their hair, well something happened to me. Suddenly, I was burning."

When his Freedom Rides took him to Mississippi, Carmichael was arrested and spent forty nine days in jail. Next, the SNCC sent Carmichael to work in Lowndes County in Alabama. This was an area where the majority of people were African Americans, but they had no political power or influence. He helped to increase the number of African Americans who were registered to vote from seventy to 2,600. This meant that there were 300 more African American voters than the number of registered white voters. Carmichael became chairman of the SNCC in 1966.

In June 1966, Carmichael joined other civil rights leaders who decided to complete James Meredith's March Against Fear. When the marchers reached Greenwood, Mississippi, Carmichael was arrested by the police. It was the twenty seventh time that Carmichael had been arrested, and when he was released he made his famous Black Power speech. He publicly criticised Martin Luther King's belief in non-violent protest, and later Carmichael joined the militant Black Panther Party.

In 1967 Carmichael and Charles Hamilton wrote the book, *Black Power*. Some civil rights activists accused Carmichael of anti-white racism, as Carmichael went on to use the slogan 'Black is Beautiful' and he encouraged African Americans to take pride in their race and colour. His supporters adopted what were known as Afro hairstyles, as well as African names, and African forms of dress.

When Carmichael opposed American involvement in the Vietnam War, his passport was confiscated for ten months. When his passport was returned, Carmichael and his first wife, Miriam Makeba, moved to Guinea in West Africa. He changed his name to Kwame Ture, and worked for Guinea's Prime Minister, Sekou Toure. In 1984, Carmichael was arrested by Guinea's new military regime and accused of plotting to overthrow the government. This time he spent three days in prison before being released without being charged.

Kwame Ture (Stokely Carmichael) died in November 1998. At the time of his death Ture had not played any part in African American affairs for more than twenty years.

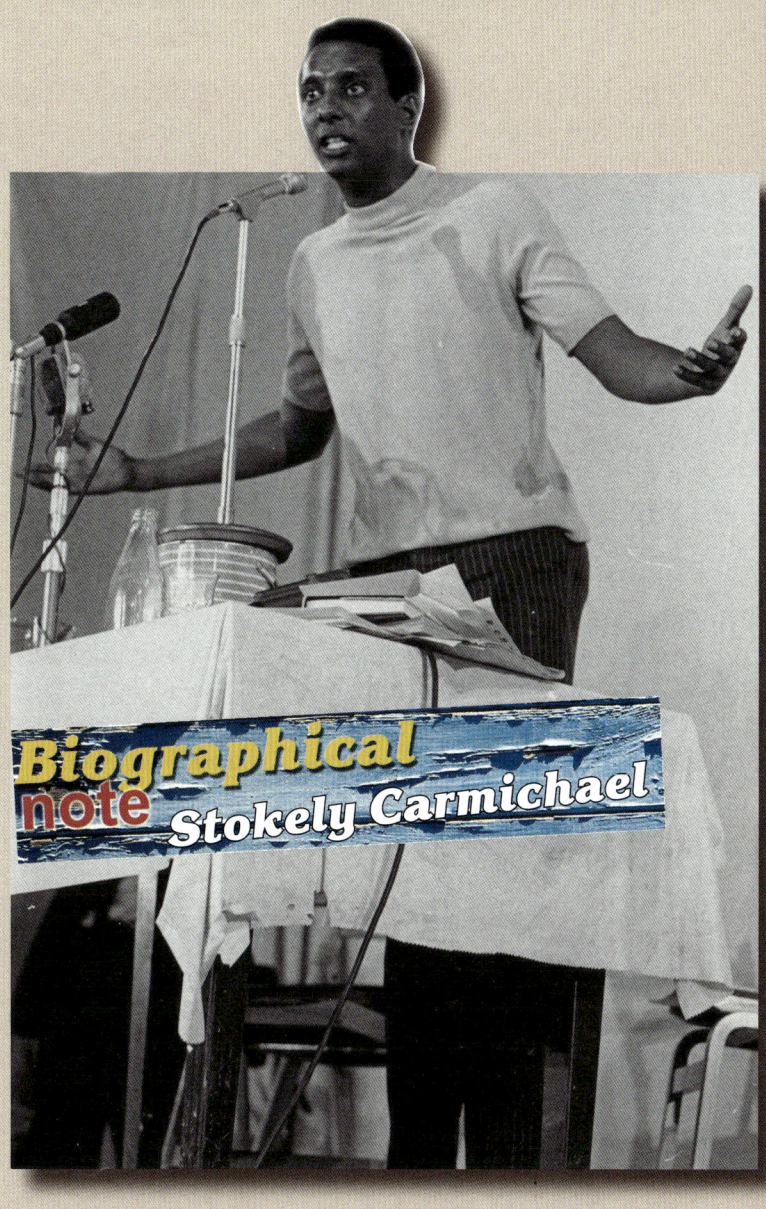

Biographical note: Stokely Carmichael

sented racial pride and African American leadership of political organisations that were prepared to fight for civil rights throughout the USA. To Whites and those African Americans who believed in non-violent protest the slogan represented a form of racism that would divide African Americans from each other, and from other Americans.

THE BLACK PANTHERS

In 1966 police brutality against African Americans led Huey Newton and Bobby Seale to set up the Black Panther Party in Oakland, California. This party was supposed to be an African American self-defence group within the Oakland ghetto, but soon it attracted national attention when a group of Black Panthers invaded the California State legislature or parliament. The Black Panthers wanted to protest against a new gun-control law that was being discussed.

The Black Panthers were popular with young African Americans and most American cities had a branch of the party by 1968. In the ghettos the Black Panthers organised self-help for African American communities including free breakfast clubs for children, and free health clinics. However, the Black Panthers lost many of their supporters among African Americans and sympathetic Whites because of their members' violent actions which included many gunfights with the police.

In 1969, twenty seven Black Panthers, including two party leaders, were shot dead by the police in several gunfights, and over 700 were arrested for various offences. The US government claimed that the Black Panthers were involved in organising terrorist acts against the US federal government. The federal law enforcement agency, the FBI, spied on the two best known Black Panther leaders, Huey Newton and Bobby Seale who, together with another party leader, Eldridge Cleaver, were charged with murder at different times. The Black Panther Party finally broke up in 1972.

Black Panthers marching in New York in July 1968 to protest at the trial of one of their members, Huey P Newton. Newton was later convicted for the manslaughter of an Oakland policeman.

Biographical note: Bobby Seale

Bobby Seale was born in Texas in 1936. During World War II, the Seale family moved to Oakland, California. When he left high school, Seale joined the US Air Force. In 1962 Seale attended Merritt College in Oakland, California. It was when he was a student that he became active in the civil rights movement.

In 1966 Seale and Huey Newton set up the Black Panther Party. In 1968 Seale was charged with trying to start a riot during the Democratic Party's National Convention to select the Party's presidential candidate. He was found guilty and sentenced to four years in prison. While in prison Seale was charged with murdering a former Black Panther suspected of being a police informer. The trial ended with the jury unable to reach a verdict, so the judge ordered all charges against Seale to be dropped.

After he was released from prison in 1972, Seale decided to concentrate on mainstream politics. In 1973 Seale ran for Mayor of Oakland but he came second. Since that defeat, Seale has worked on a variety of community projects and has published several books, including his autobiography.

The Black Panthers put forward a Ten Point Programme which represented their view of how to help African Americans in the ghettos.

Ten Point Programme

1. We want freedom. We want power to determine the destiny of our black community.
2. We want full employment for our people.
3. We want an end to the robbery of our black community by the racist government of the USA.
4. We want decent housing.
5. We want education for our people. We want education that teaches us our true history and our role in present day society.
6. We want all black men to be exempt from military service.
7. We want an immediate end to police brutality and murder of black people.
8. We want freedom for all black men held in American jails.
9. When black people are brought to trial let them be tried in a court with a jury of black people.
10. We want land, bread, housing, education, clothing, justice and peace.

Biographical note: Eldridge Cleaver

Eldridge Cleaver was born in Arkansas in 1935. His family moved to Los Angeles and as a young man Cleaver was arrested for possessing and selling marijuana. He was sentenced to thirty months in prison. While in Soledad Prison, Cleaver became interested in politics. He was released in 1957 only to be arrested and charged with attempted murder. He was found guilty and was sentenced to two to fourteen years in prison. In San Quentin, Cleaver began reading about the civil rights movement and the ideas of Malcolm X.

On his release from prison in 1966, Cleaver joined the Black Panthers and soon became one of the party's leaders. He published his autobiography called *Soul on Ice* in 1968. In that same year, Cleaver was with seven other Black Panthers when a gunfight broke out between the Panthers and the Oakland police. Cleaver and another Panther called Hutton took shelter in the basement of a nearby building. Surrounded by police the two Panthers decided to surrender. Cleaver was wounded in the leg and so Hutton said that he would go out first. As he came out of the building with his hands in the air Hutton was shot twelve times by the police and killed.

Cleaver was arrested and charged with attempted murder. Before his trial, Cleaver fled to Mexico. Next he moved to Cuba, before moving on to Algeria. Cleaver returned to the USA in 1975 where he was arrested and put on trial for his part in the 1968 gunfight. He was sentenced to five years' probation and 2,000 hours of community service.

In 1994 Cleaver was seriously injured while he was attempting to buy cocaine from a drug dealer. In 1998 he appeared in court charged with burglary and cocaine possession. He died in May 1998.

Free at Last?

14

Free at Last?

What you will learn

Intermediate 2

- The importance of the Civil Rights Act (1968) for the civil rights struggle

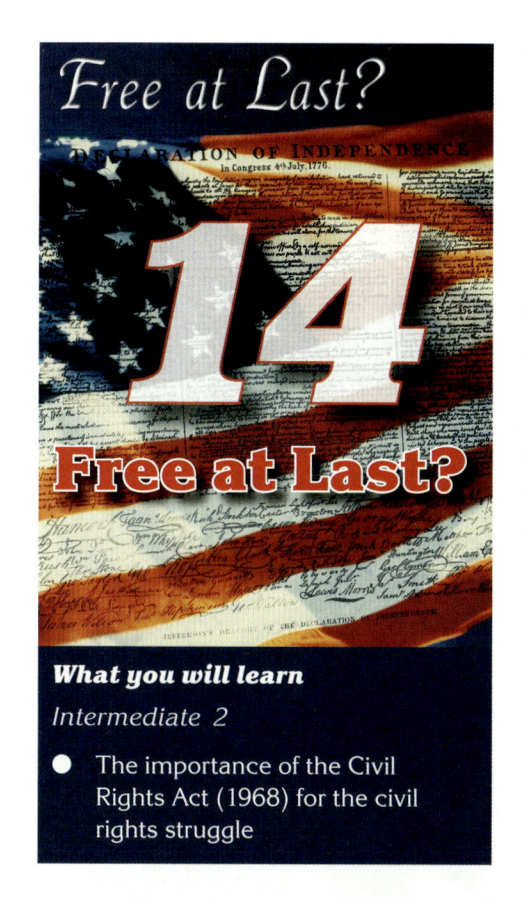

THE DEATH OF MARTIN LUTHER KING

In March 1968, the Reverend James Lawson of Memphis, Tennessee, invited Martin Luther King to lend his support to local African American workers who were on strike. These sanitation workers in Memphis had gone on strike to force their employers to recognise their trade union and to win a pay rise. On 28 March, King led a public demonstration in downtown Memphis to publicise the strikers' case. The rally was poorly organised and gang members and other African American youths at the back of the crowd smashed windows and looted shops.

King decided to remain in Memphis to assist the campaigners. On 3 April, King spoke at a public meeting in the Mason temple where he encouraged African Americans in Memphis to work together to defeat racism and injustice. He ended his speech by saying that he was not worried by the many death threats which he had received when in Tennessee. He said:

"Well, I don't know what will happen now. We've got some difficult days ahead. But it doesn't matter with me now. Because I've been to the mountaintop and I don't mind. Like anybody, I would like to live a long life. Longevity has its place. But I'm not concerned about that now. I just want to do God's will. And he's allowed me to go up to the mountain. And I've looked over. And I've seen the Promised Land. I may not get there with you. But I want you to know tonight that we as a people will get to the Promised Land. And I'm happy, tonight. I'm not worried about anything. I'm not fearing any man. Mine eyes have seen the glory of the coming of the Lord."

The next day King was shot and killed by an assassin as he stood on his room balcony in the Lorraine Motel in Memphis. King's violent death, apparently shot dead by a lone white gunman (James Earl Ray), sparked off riots in African American ghettos across the USA.

Martin Luther King's funeral procession, 1968

THE CIVIL RIGHTS ACT (1968)

Martin Luther King's funeral took place on 9 April at the Ebenezer Church in Atlanta, Georgia. On 10 April, the US Congress responded to King's death by passing a new *Civil Rights Act*. The new law was supposed to provide greater protection for civil rights workers in the South, and contained a section designed to end segregation in housing which had been too controversial to introduce up to that point.

The Act also included anti-riot measures designed to tackle what many Whites saw as the growing menace of lawlessness in so many African American communities. (The new law made it an offence to move from one state to another with the intention of inciting a riot.) It was clear that President Johnson believed that most Whites were losing patience with the militant tactics of African American protesters, and he wanted to be seen to be acting to put an end to the riots.

The *Civil Rights Act* of 1968 had little or no impact on the struggle for civil rights. The death of Martin Luther King and this new law marked the end of the direct action phase of the civil rights struggle.

WHAT NEXT?

Black Power encouraged other ethnic groups to see themselves as victims of white racist oppression. Hispanic activists formed 'Beret' movements based on the Black Panthers, and demanded equal rights for Mexican Americans. Native American groups supported 'Red Power' and organised a series of protests against the poverty and hardships of life on Native American reservations. These protests culminated in a group of Native Americans seizing control of the historic site of Wounded Knee where US soldiers had massacred a group of Native Americans in 1890. This event gained nationwide publicity for these Native American protesters.

In US prisons thousands of African American convicts listened to Black Power ideas. Prisoners in Soledad and San Quentin were educated in the ideas of the Black Panthers and other militant African Americans. Some convicts wrote about their experiences outside and

(continued on page 72)

By 1968 African Americans were dominating major American sports in a way that no one could have predicted at the beginning of the decade. In that year, half of all professional basketball players, one-third of all major league baseball players, and one-third of all American Football players were African Americans. In 1968 Arthur Ashe became the first African American winner of the US Open men's singles tennis title. At the 1968 Olympic Games in Mexico City, athletics gold medallist Tommy Smith and silver medallist John Carlos gave the Black Power salute when the American national anthem was played at their medal ceremony, to the great annoyance of many Americans of every race and colour. Both athletes were suspended from the US Olympic team.

FACTFILE: African Americans in sport

Biographical note: George Wallace

George Wallace was born in Alabama in 1919. A farmer's son, Wallace and his brothers Jack and Gerald, and his sister Marianne, attended local schools and helped out on the farm. When his father died in 1937, Wallace began to work his way through law school by boxing professionally, waiting on tables, serving as a kitchen helper, and driving a taxi. He graduated in 1942 and following a brief period in the US Air Force (he was given a medical discharge), Wallace returned to Alabama where he served as an Assistant Attorney General for the state.

In 1947, George Wallace was elected to the state legislature as a Democrat. In 1958, Wallace tried to become the Democratic candidate for state Governor. He received more than a quarter of a million votes, placing him second to the successful candidate, John Patterson. Patterson was openly racist and accepted the support of the Ku Klux Klan; Wallace had accepted support from the NAACP.

Wallace resumed his legal career but formed a plan to achieve his aim of becoming Governor of Alabama. His views on race relations and segregation underwent a dramatic change. He made it clear that he supported the segrgationists in order to win the support of white racists who felt threatened by the African American Civil Rights activists. At the election in 1962, Wallace received the largest vote ever achieved by a candidate for governor in Alabama up to that time.

Wallace's first term as Governor of Alabama was marked by an increase in racial tension as the African American campaign for civil rights grew more aggressive. Among the major incidents of Wallace's first administration were racial demonstrations in Birmingham and Montgomery, and the desegregation of schools in Macon County. In 1964, he entered the presidential primaries in Wisconsin, Maryland and Indiana as a possible candidate for the Democrats, receiving 43% of the vote. However, his party stood by President Johnson as its candidate, and he won the presidential election for the Democrats.

In September 1965, Wallace tried to have an amendment made to state law to allow a sitting governor to run for a second term in office. This move was not successful, so Wallace persuaded his wife Lurleen to run as his stand-in. The main opponent to his wife for the governorship was killed when his small private plane crashed while he was campaigning in mountainous northern Alabama. Wallace's wife served one term as Governor of Alabama.

In 1970, George Wallace was elected as Governor of Alabama for a second time.

In May 1972, while campaigning in Maryland to become a presidential candidate, he was shot by a would-be assassin, Arthur Bremer. As a result of the assassination attempt, Wallace was paralysed in both legs and this ended his hopes of becoming US President. He returned to his duties as Governor of Alabama.

An amendment to the Alabama state constitution allowed Wallace to remain in office for another term as Governor. In 1982, Wallace successfully stood as candidate for the governorship for a final time. This time, a large number of African American voters in Alabama supported Wallace. For someone who had been the chief spokesperson for Alabama's segregationists for so many years, this represented a complete turnabout in his political career. Wallace relied on the so-called 'Wallace Coalition' which included trade unions and African American organisations, for much of his support, and this highlights how much had changed since the violent events of the 1960s. Ill health forced George Wallace to retire from politics, and he died in Montgomery, Alabama, on 13 September 1998.

George Wallace, the Democratic Governor of Alabama, standing in the doorway of the administrative building of the University of Alabama in Tuscaloosa in order to prevent two African American students from entering. Wallace had run for Governor with the slogan 'Segregation Forever'.

inside prison, and about their treatment at the hands of racist police officers and prison warders. The suspicious death of the writer George Jackson, who had become a well-known figure among African American prisoners, led to violent protests in many prisons. At Attica prison in New York State over forty prison guards and prisoners died in a riot.

AFFIRMATIVE ACTION

In 1972, the US Congress passed two laws. One was the Equal Employment Opportunity Act (EEO), and the other was the Equal Opportunity Act. Known as 'affirmative action' laws, both of these Acts made it necessary for all US government agencies, state governments, local governments, and public institutions to hire more African Americans, as well as hire from any other groups facing discrimination. Any government agencies or private companies that received money from the US government were required to ensure that a percentage of any goods and services they used were from African American-owned, female-owned, or other minority-owned companies.

Within a few years affirmative action had been so successful in forcing open job opportunities for African Americans and other groups facing discrimination that its critics claimed that job discrimination no longer existed. They claimed that setting aside a certain number of jobs for particular groups was reverse discrimination against other groups, such as white males who were often better qualified than those who had been denied jobs. Supporters of affirmative action said that it was necessary if African Americans, who had suffered from poverty and a lack of opportunities for many years, were to enjoy their fair share of available job opportunities.

By 1982 there were over 300,000 American businesses owned by African Americans. In that same year the US Congress voted to extend the Voting Rights Act (1965) for another twenty five years. However, in the 1980s President Ronald Reagan (Republican) then President George Bush (Republican) spoke out against civil rights reforms and affirmative action. Both Presidents appointed judges to federal courts, including the Supreme Court, who were opposed to affirmative action.

President George Bush signed a Civil Rights Act (1991) that limited the scope and extent of affirmative action. In that same year, a witness used his video camera to record four white police officers brutally beating an African American motorist as he was being arrested in Los Angeles. When the police officers were found not guilty of the charges made against them, the worst riots in US history took place in Los Angeles.

In 1995 the US Supreme Court, which was now dominated by judges appointed by Reagan and Bush, decided to reverse its decision on the legality of the affirmative action programmes. The Supreme Court announced that most affirmative action programmes were illegal, and only a few programmes could be allowed, so long as they were aimed at specific cases of discrimination, and only in particular areas of employment.

THE MILLION MAN MARCH, 1996

In October 1996, the African American minister and controversial spokesperson on behalf of many African American causes, the Reverend Louis Farrakhan, urged African American men to stand up and be counted in the battles against drugs, violent crime and poverty. He asked for one million African American males to travel to Washington DC and take part in an all day event called the Million Man March. The event was supported by African American politicians, religious leaders and artists from all over the country, and one of the main speakers was Rosa Parks. The battle for African American civil rights was not yet won, more than fifty years after it had begun in the aftermath of World War II.